Praise for Alan Carroll and *Th*

"Alan Carroll's teachings on communications have been instrumental to our success. These methods really work. They aren't merely training; Alan shows us how to develop new habits that have profoundly impacted our ability to communicate with our customers."

—Sam Alkharrat

Managing Director, Cisco Systems

"There is no one better in the business than Alan Carroll. His program is unique, he has a passion for the art and science of presentation skills, and his results speak for themselves. I have been to countless media and presentation skills training classes, and Alan's has always stood atop them all. I utilize the things I have learned in his training sessions to this day."

—Bill Nuti

Chairman and CEO, NCR

"Alan Carroll's seminars have been the most powerful and influential training sessions that I have provided to my colleagues, improving their performance and helping them to achieve their full potential. His new book captures the essence of this experience, and should help anyone for whom good communication is an essential part of his or her professional success."

—Jonathan White

Chief Information Officer, Pfizer, Inc.

"The most important skill that knowledge workers in the IT industry must have today is the ability to manage a customer conversation. Clear, articulate communications and impeccable presentation delivery are often the difference in making the customer connection and closing the deal or simply leading with influence. Alan has coached thousands of professionals through the communications 'mind block'—transforming nervous presentations into memorable performances. Learn here the skills that will let you confidently own the room (and own time and space), and approach each speaking opportunity with a new presence that will guarantee you hit the target every time."

—Randy L Wood III
VP of Worldwide Sales, Agent Logic, Inc.

The Broadband Connection

The Art of Delivering a Winning IT Presentation

Alan Carroll

BENBELLA BOOKS, INC.

Dallas, TX

PowerPoint®, Holiday Inn®, QuickTime® movies, Sanford Mr. Sketch®, and Coca-Cola® are all registered trademarks.

BENBELLA

BenBella Books, Inc.
6440 N. Central Expressway, Suite 503
Dallas, TX 75206
www.benbellabooks.com
Send feedback to feedback@benbellabooks.com

Printed in the United States of America
10 9 8 7 6 5 4 3 2 1

Library of Congress Cataloging-in-Publication Data is available for this title.
978-1933771-90-8

Proofreading by Stacia Seaman and Erica Lovett
Cover design by Laura Watkins
Text design and composition by PerfecType, Nashville, TN
Printed by Bang Printing
Indexing by Shoshana Hurwitz

Distributed by Perseus Distribution
perseusdistribution.com

To place orders through Perseus Distribution:
Tel: 800-343-4499
Fax: 800-351-5073
E-mail: orderentry@perseusbooks.com

Significant discounts for bulk sales are available. Please contact Glenn Yeffeth at glenn@benbellabooks.com or (214) 750-3628.

Acknowledgment

There are three groups I want to acknowledge for the wonderful contributions they have given to me in my development of *The Broadband Connection*: First, and most importantly, the thousands of students over the last thirty years that I have had the privilege of training and being trained by. Secondly, the spiritual teachers Sai Baba, Sri Aurobindo, Old Chinese and modern day transformational masters Werner Erhard and, most recently, Eckhart Tolle, whose illumination has been dazzling. And I especially want to thank my wife, Donna; the twins, Alan and Jennifer; and Shelly for their support through this process.

Contents

Introduction

The purpose of this book is to share with you the tools and insights I have discovered after almost thirty years of teaching presentation/communication skills worldwide, in order to support your transformation from a so-so presenter to a "superstar." Although most of the people I have coached are from the IT* world, the presentation tools and insights discussed are applicable to anyone who has to stand up and talk in front of audiences.

I have had the privilege of working with thousands of IT professionals in over fifty countries and representing many diversified cultures. And the one fact that is readily apparent is that cross-culturally our similarities far outweigh our differences. The blocks and barriers that stop an engineer or account manager in Tokyo from having full self-expression and presence are the same that block the engineer or account manager in New York, London, Moscow, New

---

* The term IT stands for Information Technology and is defined as the study, design, development, implementation, support, or management of computer-based information systems, particularly software applications, networks, and computer hardware.

Delhi, or Johannesburg. We may speak different languages. We may have been raised in different cultures. But the essence of our humanity, being, and spirit are all the same.

The key element in this transformation for any person is the ability to stay in present time while delivering your communication and not get distracted or seduced by the data. IT professionals are masters at the ability to acquire the knowledge but are often challenged by the ability to take that knowledge or content and effectively deliver it to the audience. By diminishing the blocks and barriers that stop your full self-expression and clarity, you increase your ability to stay in present time, which I refer to as the Broadband Connection. When the blocks and barriers begin to dissolve, your Being, which is right underneath the surface of consciousness, can begin to emerge and illuminate space. You then have a greater connection to this moment of now and in this new state of consciousness will have the maximum capability to be of service and contribute to the audience.

This light of illumination, which is analogous to watching high-definition television for the first time, captivates an audience. They aren't able to take their attention off the presenter. They are inspired and appreciative that someone is actually taking the time to consciously encapsulate the thought and project it across the space with the intention that it be absorbed and understood.

My own ability to be in present time in front of an audience was developed through years of practice, the opportunity to teach others, and the inspiration of some brilliant guides who pointed the way.

In my early development back in the '70s Werner Erhard was a brilliant light in my life. I had unknowingly been protecting myself from being present with the audience, erroneously thinking that if I was fully present I would be psychologically vulnerable, which would lead to rejection. Through Werner's training I was able to surrender, take a leap of faith into the unknown, and risk what I thought would be total annihilation in front of the audience.

But to my amazement I wasn't annihilated. Quite the opposite. I discovered a space of awareness or consciousness that I had never tasted before. The space of freedom. Freedom to be myself. Freedom to tell the truth about my experience of life. Freedom from being suppressed by what I thought the audience would think about me. And one of the most wonderful and unexpected gifts I received was the ability to generate compassion for myself and others.

The heart and soul of *The Broadband Connection* was and continues to be inspired by Eckhart Tolle and his insight into consciousness. His understanding of presence and the ability to clearly deliver that understanding to others through his words and videos is a gift to the world. For example, he makes a simple distinction that there are only two things in this world: space and things in space.

When I hear ideas like these a part of me gets very excited because I may not have the direct experience of what the teacher is talking about but I intuitively sense that it points to a profound truth in consciousness. Then I am blessed with the opportunity to take the idea into training rooms around the world to see if it aids in diminishing the blocks and barriers that stop my students from being in present time and maintaining their own broadband connection to the audience. And over the years a process has emerged that supports students in transforming their ability to be clear, confident, and powerful presenters. They now experience that standing in front of audiences is not something to dread but rather one of the best and most fun parts of their job. Their audiences look at them and exclaim, "Wow, that looks like a superstar!"

With the Warmest of Regards,

Alan
Saudi Arabia
January 2009

1

Wireless Packet
Delivery

When an IT professional stands up in front of an audience to deliver a presentation, you can refer to him or her as the sender of communication and the audience as the receivers of communication. In IT terminology, the sender would be the source router and the audience would be the destination routers.

Given that there are no wires connecting the presenter to the audience, the presenter is transmitting his or her communication packets and space packets over a wireless local area network.

This chapter is intended to clarify the distinction between communication packets and space packets and how to improve the quality and effectiveness of your delivery as a presenter.

Almost all the packets the IT professional delivers are communication packets and contain only one element—data. In my experience, the vast majority of IT professionals could teasingly be referred to as unconscious, low-intentioned, and ineffective "data dumpers."

A low-intentioned data dumper is someone who just drops the data in the space with little or no intention that the audience will actually understand it. The data dumper is not present. He or she has not formed a conscious connection with the audience, is not grounded, and has no interest in packaging the data in a manner that leaves a lasting impression with the audience.

In an ideal situation, the communication flow would contain two kinds of packets: communication and space packets.

Communication packets include several components: data, voice (which may contain emotional tone), video, and sometimes mass.*

Although space packets, which can also be referred to in the IP voice world as interframe gaps, contain only space, they are extremely important because they represent the portal through which a broadband, present-time connection is made with the audience.

IT presenters who are striving to present at the highest level of effectiveness should attempt to integrate both communication and space packets into their presentations. However, most IT professionals are so focused on the data that they include few or no space packets in their delivery. As a result, they remain disconnected from both present time and their audience. The benefits of integrating

---

* Mass: Most presentations employ PowerPoint® slides, whiteboards, and flip charts, which are two-dimensional tools, to explain abstract concepts. One of the barriers to clarity is that people don't have enough mass around the concept. *Mass* is the use of physical items in the space. As a presenter, you should always be looking for mass to help the audience understand abstract IT concepts.

space packets and communication packets into a delivery can be enormous.

Let's explore the distinction between communication packets and space packets in more detail. The ideal mix of components in a communication packet is 7 percent data, 38 percent voice, and 55 percent video. Voice and video together compose 93 percent of the communication packet.

What is video? Video is the ability to use your body to embody your thoughts.

When you embody the thought with physical expression, the audience not only hears the data but *sees* the data. It is as if the audience is at the movies watching a professional actor delivering his or her lines. Mimes—who only use their bodies, never their voices, to communicate—are great examples of the outstanding use of video.

You rarely see video components in IT professionals' delivery. They are so focused on the data that they are unable to create the space even to think about including video in the packet. And yet, video should represent 55 percent of the communication packet because it is a key tool in increasing your effectiveness; in this case, a picture really is worth a thousand words.

Your effectiveness can be measured by how memorable you are in front of an audience.

Here's an interesting definition of memory: linear, sequential moments of *now* stored in your internal database. You could say that each moment of *now* from the beginning to the end of your life is recorded in this linear set of frames. The frame contains several parts: the video picture of the experience, the sound track, the emotions, and even the smells associated with the experience.

When you ask people to remember something, they often first remember the video image. Once they have a picture of that image in their mind's eye, it increases their probability of also remembering the sound track or data.

Smell is so powerful it can trigger a memory that takes you back to a moment that may have occurred twenty years ago. You see in your mind a picture of the place; you remember the thoughts and emotions, even though it was two decades in the past.

One would assume the goal of most IT professionals' presentations is to be effective. This means you actually want your audience to remember what you are talking about. Research suggests that most audiences remember 10 percent of the data twenty-four hours after attending the presentation. This is not effective and suggests that the presenter was not delivering the message in a memorable fashion.

One way to become more memorable is to integrate video gestures into all your communication packets. Using your hands and arms provides most video images. However, you can also use your whole body to create the video impression for the audience. The more vivid and powerful the image is, the more lasting the impression it makes on the audience.

Unfortunately, powerful and vivid video images are rare in IT professionals' presentations.

Why?

In order to create a powerful vivid video image, presenters must be trained in the delivery skill, committed to the data, and equally committed to helping the audience understand the data.

My observation has been that the average IT professional is brilliant in mastering the acquisition of data but still needs to improve his or her ability to communicate the data clearly so the audience understands it. Presenters need to shift from a self-absorbed attitude—"I'm just doing my job"—to an attitude focused on contribution and service to the audience.

Generating high-quality video images requires presenters to control the time and space in which they work. They need to be very grounded and anchored in present time in order to maintain a broadband connection to the audience. The anchored broadband connection will allow them to create more space packets. And, in that conscious environment, they can manifest their intention more fully, as well as develop and sustain the video image they want to transmit to the audience.

By giving yourself time, you create the space to think about what to do with your body to convey your thought to the audience in the form of a video image. The more you practice using your body to transmit video images, the more natural it becomes. Eventually, creating video images will be second nature and you will not have to think about it consciously anymore.

It is my experience that almost every sentence an IT professional delivers has the possibility of containing video components. Let's say you were thinking of the word *large*. To create a video image for *large,* you would open and extend your arms. If you thought the word *small*, you would bring your arms and hands close together. If you thought the words *over there*, you would extend your arm toward another section of the room. If you said *the packets move from one point of the network to another point on the network*, you could move your whole body from one point in the room to another.

(For more information on creating video images, visit www.carroll train.com, where you can see me demonstrate a wide variety of video images using hands, arms, and body.)

Now, let's look at the verbal or voice component of the packet, which makes up 38 percent of the delivery.

Many IT professionals speak in a single tone of voice: a mono-tone. A monotone delivery lacks life and vitality. It is not inspiring and may bore the listener.

Your voice is like a musical instrument. It can play a wide variety of notes. You can change the speed of your voice, that is, the baud rate; you can change the volume and the cadence, as well as the inflection or emphasis of your speaking. All these changes can make listening to you more interesting. You can also change the pitch of your voice, making it higher or lower. However, in my experience, changing pitch isn't appropriate in professional IT presentations.

Just as each sentence you deliver has its video possibility, it also has the possibility of making vocal changes, which will improve your delivery.

If your body is not being used consciously, your voice will lack full expression and be monotonous. However, when you consciously include your body in the communication, your voice will register vocal changes, which compels the audience to pay attention.

> **Coaching Tip**
>
> Your voice is closely connected to your body movements. If you use your body to create video images, your voice will automatically follow and flow with the rhythms of your physical expression.

This idea is analogous to the performance of an Indian snake charmer. As the fakir plays the flute, the cobra rises from the basket and appears to be swaying back and forth, mesmerized by the music. As you add vocal variety to the delivery of your data, you charm the audience into paying attention. A flat monotonous delivery is dull and lacks the charismatic power of attraction.

(Visit my Web site to hear and watch me deliver data using my voice and body.)

Many IT professionals typically don't include vocal skills in their communication packets for several reasons:

Conscious / Awake

Wonderland, Being, Stillness,
No Resistance, Spaciousness, No Thoughts,
Free, Clear, Light, Control, Present,
Relax

Broadband

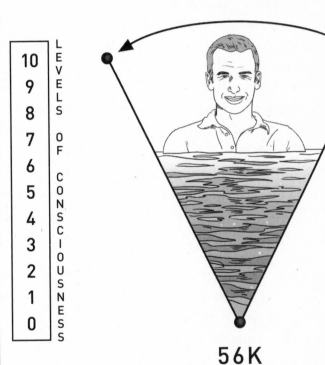

LEVELS OF CONSCIOUSNESS

10
9
8
7
6
5
4
3
2
1
0

56K

Data Land, Ego, Resistance, Dense,
Thoughts, Prison, Foggy, Heavy,
No Control, Not Present

Unconscious / Asleep

- The first reason is simply a lack of training. They have never received the coaching needed to acquire these skills.
- Second, they are not forming a present-time, conscious, broadband connection with the audience.
- Third, they are focused on the content rather than the space from which the content emerges. In order to execute effective voice changes and create high-impact video images, you need to increase your level of consciousness in the space. As your conscious awareness, comfort, and confidence increase, you become increasingly able to create space packets between your communication packets, which gives you the time to think about how best to project your next communication into the space of the room.

This ability to create space packets consciously moves the presenter into present time and establishes a broadband connection to the audience.

Most people have little consciousness awareness, which gives them only a connection comparable to a 56k dial-up connection to the audience. A 56k dial-up connection severely limits your ability to create clear video images and make vocal changes.

- Fourth, they do not intend the audience to duplicate or understand the data. If they did, they would find ways to express the data to maximize comprehension and retention.
- Fifth, they are not committed to the data. They do not invest the data with energy and passion, so they do not commit their voice and body to it. As a result, the audience asks, "Why should I be committed and buy this solution if the person delivering the data is not committed?"

Obviously, those who are committed to the data are more apt to engage their voice and body in conveying it. However, IT presenters rarely come out from behind their firewalls and expose themselves both vocally and physically to the audience. In contrast, by delivering your communication from in front of your firewall, you will have a greater presence and the power to manifest your message.

The firewall distinction is addressed in detail in chapter two.

So far, we have looked at the video and voice parts of the communication packet. Now, let's explore another piece—the data. The data is the heart and soul of the presentation, although it represents only 7 percent of the total communication packet.

The data resides in three locations: first, in the internal database of the presenter; second, in the external database such as the PowerPoint slides; and third, for participation purposes, in the database of the audience.

The principal goal for the presenter is to transfer as much data as is appropriate to the audience effectively with the intention of helping them understand the information.

The major problem with some IT presentations is that they dump a huge quantity of data into the space with little or no intention that the audience will understand the concepts. An IT managing director I met in the Middle East referred to this as *nuking* the audience. Another referred to it as *dropping data bombs* on them.

Sadly, it seems to be the norm that the presenter doesn't think it's his or her job to help the audience understand the data. The presenter's only responsibility is to fly in, show up, throw the data out there, and leave. This sort of presenter believes it's the audience's job to make sense of the data that was dumped on them.

This is not effective. The definition of communication is transmitting information from a sender to a receiver with the intention that the receiver understands the data. When you actually connect

WIRELESS PACKET DELIVERY

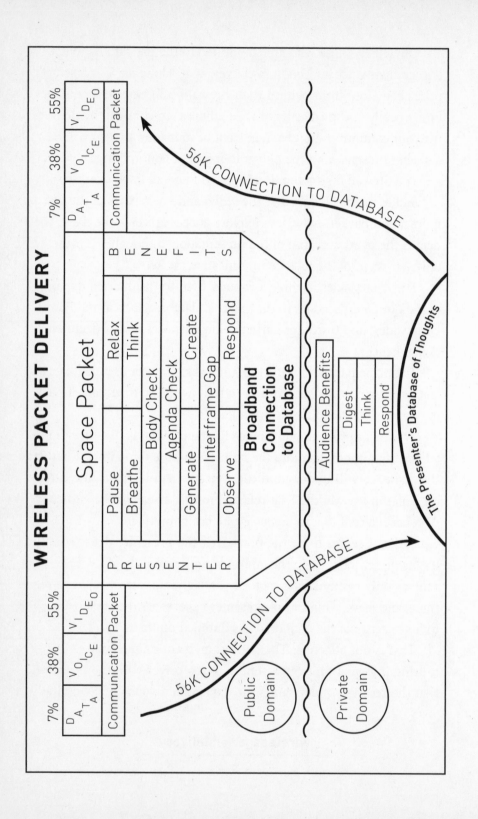

with the intention that your audience will understand the data, you'll make a major transformational shift in your skills as a professional presenter. You will move from being a data dumper to being a professional who is regarded as one of the best in the industry, a genuine star. You will feel the power that comes from a successful presentation and the audience will enjoy a genuine, informative show.

Now, let's address the process of communicating a packet across the wireless space from the sender to the receiver with special emphasis on using space packets between the communication packets.

In the ideal situation, you start your presentation/conversation by diving into your database of knowledge and pulling up a thought. You encapsulate the thought with a word, then add a video image, vocal tones, and maybe some physical objects. You consciously project the encapsulated thought across the space to the receiver. Once that burst of communication is complete, you pause and allow the audience to digest, process, think about, and absorb the data. During this pause, you relax your body, take a breath, and think about your next communication packet.

Alice Bailey, the author of more than a dozen books on spiritual development, describes the speech process beautifully: "The purpose of speech is to clothe thought and thus make our thoughts available to others. When we speak we evoke a thought and make it present, and we bring that which is concealed within us into audible expression."

As I emphasized, the ability to create space packets between the communication packets is a critical skill for the IT professional presenter. Just as there are communication packets, there are also space packets. Space packets are the silence or pauses between the communication packets. When you talk to the audience, you are delivering not only data but space as well. And yet, when you watch IT presenters, you'll see that few have little if any intention of consciously creating space packets. The vast majority focus their consciousness on content rather than on the space from which the content flows.

In order to create space packets, you need to be in present time with the audience. You cannot have one foot in the future (that is, be inside your head thinking about what you are going to say next) while keeping the other foot in the past (thinking about what you just said). You need to have both feet in present time. In the moment of delivery, the past and future temporarily disappear. In this moment of now, or frame, you can create a communication that will make a difference, be of service, and contribute to the audience's knowledge and understanding.

(Your understanding of the concept of time and maintaining a broadband connection to the audience is critical to your success as a presenter and will be fully discussed in chapter six, which focuses on consciousness.)

One critical mistake almost every presenter makes is to follow the first communication packets with another burst of packets without giving the audience a chance to digest what they have already heard. This failure to deliver space packets creates congestion, overloads the receivers' buffers, and reduces throughput, thereby diminishing the effectiveness of the communication. The extraordinary communicators, like actors, have conscious control of their baud rate and can consciously create space packets between their communication packets.

Why is it so difficult for presenters to create these space packets? Mostly because they have never made the distinction between content consciousness and space consciousness. Their attention is on the content itself, rather than on creating space between the content. Eckhart Tolle states that there are two types of consciousness:

content consciousness and space consciousness. They both work together to produce an effective presentation. However, IT presenters are almost always focused on content rather than space.

Presenters who are fixated on the data are not present in the room. They are barely connected to the audience. They have a 56k connection rather than a present-time, broadband connection to the audience. They have no presence. To put it another way, they suffer from data addiction and would rather make love to the data than be present to the audience. If they are not connected or consciously present in the room, where are they? They are in a place I call *Data Land*.

Data Land is in a space outside of present time. It is a world in which unconsciousness rules and the power to communicate is weak and ineffective. It is a world in which you are unaware of your physical body.

Fortunately, when you begin to shift your consciousness from the data to the space between packets, you return to being present in the room and can establish a broadband connection to the audience.

You will immediately notice a major improvement in your delivery because you are no longer focused on the object/data/content but rather on the space itself. This is the exact opposite of the way the vast majority of IT professionals make presentations.

When done properly, you are not delivering data; you are delivering space. When you begin to deliver space, the quality and effectiveness of your speaking increases because, in addition to maintaining a broadband connection to the audience, you will be relaxed throughout the entire conversation.

Another reason it's difficult to create space packets is because we have been conditioned to feel very strange and uncomfortable if we pause when standing in front of the audience. Part of the discomfort comes from an assumption you make about how the audience will react. If you don't speak, you suspect that they will think you have lost your train of thought or you are unprofessional and not a very good speaker. However, the opposite is true. When you can stand in stillness, it sends a non-verbal message to the audience that you are not afraid of silence and you are not afraid of the audience. You, not the audience, are in charge of the conversation.

Developing the skill of creating space packets begins with simply being able to stop speaking and pause. Think of it as stepping on the brake to stop the car. Anyone can step on the accelerator, but very few presenters can step on the brake and pause. To put it more bluntly, the issue is not your ability to speak but rather your inability to shut up.

The benefits of pausing and creating space packets between the communication packets are enormous:

- You will make a deeper impression on the audience and therefore be more memorable.
- You will be more entertaining and put on a better show. Ben Kingsley, who won a Best Actor Oscar for his performance as Gandhi, when asked what made him such a successful actor, replied, "I am able to stand in the stillness and pause."
- You will look more professional and polished. By being able to create space packets, you will differentiate yourself and your company from your competitors. There is a saying in sales: *Differentiate or Die.* What one thing makes you different from the rest of the herd? You create space in your presentations.
- You will convey the impression of caring that the audience understands the communication by giving them time to understand an idea before going on to the next communication. They will feel enriched because you are allowing them to "eat the data food."

- The only time you can consciously relax your body is when you are not speaking. If you are not relaxed, it will send out a tense vibration to the audience and they will become uncomfortable. However, when you are relaxed, it sends out a vibration that will relax the audience. Being able to create a space packet in front of the audience is like stepping into a Jacuzzi. It is very relaxing.

I remember a physics class I took in high school in which the teacher used a fish tank full of water in one of the experiments. Two balls were suspended in the tank. One was connected to a motor, which made the ball go up and down. The second was suspended by a rubber band. When the ball connected to the motor started to move, it sent a wave through the water. The other ball was soon vibrating at the same frequency as the motorized ball; when the motorized ball was turned off, the ball on the rubber band also stopped. During a presentation, *you* are the ball with the motor. If you are relaxed, you send out a relaxed vibration; if you're tense or nervous, you send out a nervous vibration. It is only when you pause that you can relax your body.

- Energy flows smoother through a relaxed physical body. Imagine a garden hose that is crimped. The flow of water is reduced. When the garden hose is uncrimped, the flow of water increases.
- The only time you can consciously determine if you have a solid, grounded connection to the floor and release any muscle tensions is during a pause. Having your body grounded in the space has the same benefits as grounding the flow of electricity. It gives you stability and a smooth transfer of your energy to the audience. I call this a *body check*. When you first

start body checking, you become aware that your consciousness has not been connected to your body. As a presenter, you
have been unconscious of your body. But your body is the
physical machine that is delivering the communication packets and space packets. The more aware you are of the machine,
the more body control you will have, and the more effective
the delivery of the information will be.

- The only time you can take a deep broadband dive into your
database of knowledge and pull up the appropriate next
thought is during a pause. When presenters are not pausing,
they are not thinking on their feet. They are talking from surface memory or reading PowerPoint slides.

Communication that comes from the depths of your stillness has
greater impact than communication that comes from the ripples on
the surface. I refer to this as the ability to generate the conversation.
The quality or taste of data that is generated from below the surface
is far more enjoyable for the audience than data regurgitated from
sketchy surface memory.

- The only time you can take a look at your game plan for the
conversation and make sure you are still on track is when you
pause. If you use written notes, you can quickly check where
you are in the conversation.
- The only time you can take a conscious breath is when you
pause. Breathing is one of the basic ways to keep your consciousness centered and your body relaxed. You'll often notice
that when you take a deep breath, the audience breathes with
you.
- When you pause, you are not speaking, and if you are not
speaking, then you are listening. You are listening not only to

your body but to the space around you. As you become more aware of that space, you will increase your appropriateness and manifest your intention.

- During the pause, you are giving the audience a chance to absorb, digest, and appreciate the information (data food) you have served them. I call this *creating a space for understanding*.
- During the pause, you can see the space and the things in space. You can do an agenda check to see if you are covering everything.
- The ability to pause and create space allows you to think about how you want to create and package the next expression of yourself. What words, video, voice, mass, and two-dimensional tools do you want to use to get your thoughts across to the listener?

Not allowing the audience to digest the data is rude and socially inept. Because you've allowed the audience to process the data food, they will recognize you as a professional speaker who cares about their understanding of the data.

In the IT world, it is not the quality of the food but rather the quality of the service that counts. The question is "Are you delivering the data at a one-star level of service or at a five-star level of service?"

Creating space when pausing moves you toward providing a five-star level of service. Pausing before speaking creates the impression that what you say is thoughtful, which makes listeners pay more attention.

How long do you sustain the pause? Imagine your communication is like dropping a rock into a pond. The rock hits the surface of the water and sends out waves. You sustain the pause until all the waves have ceased and the quiet calm of the water has returned. The

Word Symbol

All words are symbols that represent a thought. In other words, a symbol is a thing that represents something else. For example, when we say the word *table*, we mean a flat piece of wood with four legs that we can rest things on. When you speak, you are encapsulating thoughts with word symbols and sending those symbols across the wireless space.

The accuracy of the word symbols you use is essential.

Although most people believe they have a clear understanding of the words they use, if they looked up some of these words in a dictionary, they would discover that even if their understanding is in the ballpark, it is definitely not on home plate.

Clearing yourself on the key words and acronyms you are going to use in the presentation will give you a solid foundation to stand on and confidence when delivering your data. It will also give you the advantage in managing any resistance that comes from the audience because you can bet they have not cleared themselves on the words and acronyms.

Following several steps will allow you to satisfy yourself that you are using the words correctly. First, look each of the words up in the dictionary, then look up each of the words in the definition of each word. Check for any synonyms of the word and, finally, demonstrate the word using physical objects or what I call *mass* (see footnote on page 2).

larger the rock—that is, the more significant the point—the longer the pause should be. As you move into being present with the audience, you will know how long to pause because you will be aware of the time it's taking the audience to absorb and digest your point.

Think of it like the ringing of a bell. When you strike the bell, it sends out a sound vibration. Once the sound vibration has ceased, you strike the bell again. Dropping data into the space is like striking the bell. Once the sound vibration has stopped, go ahead and drop another communication packet. The more important the point is, the louder the ring and, therefore, the longer the pause.

This completes this section on wireless communication. Your power as a speaker will increase enormously when you shift your awareness from the content to focusing on creating space packets between the communication packets. This ability is the mark of an extraordinary professional speaker.

2

Through the Firewall
and Beyond

A firewall is a network device that protects a private network from
public network attacks. Everybody in the audience, including
the presenter, has their own psychological firewalls created by their
minds.

Where Did the Firewall Come From?

We can draw an instructive analogy from dinosaurs. When a dinosaur woke up in the morning and looked out over the Jurassic plain,
it might have seen either dinosaurs that were larger than itself or
dinosaurs that were smaller. If it saw a dinosaur that was larger, its

reptilian brain would tell it to turn around and run away. If it saw a smaller dinosaur, its brain would tell it to attack and have breakfast. Therefore, one of the primary design functions of the reptilian brain comes down to one word: *survival*.

Millions of years later, our brains have evolved. The human brain now has three parts: an outer cortex, a mid-brain, and a reptilian brain, which to this very day is still concerned about survival and the survival of whatever *it* considers itself to be. Understanding the *it* in *whatever it considers itself to be* is critical if you ever want to escape from the prison of your mind and experience life on the other side of the firewall.

In using the pronoun *it*, I am referring to psychological concepts such as *I, me, mind, ego, my story, myself, my interpretation, my beliefs, my database of thoughts, my point of view, my little story of me*, etc.

When you are born, your database of knowledge is empty. Thereafter, life becomes a conditioning process of filling your database with thoughts, education, and experiences. The thoughts and experiences you have depend on the environment into which you are born and the life experiences to which you are exposed.

As a child, your awareness of this conditioning process is negligible and you really have little if any choice about what is being programmed into your database. For example, you are told your name, family, nationality, religion, tribe, sex, etc. You agree with these labels automatically. And, once you agree, they become the things you consider yourself to be. They become the *I*, the *me*, the *ego*, the *mind*.

You are also programmed with a language, which are the word symbols or protocols your culture uses to communicate. For example, you asked your mother, "What is that?" and she said, "A tree." And now, for the rest of your life, when you see an object that has a trunk and leaves, you *know* it's a tree. It cannot show up in your conditioned conceptual reality as anything other than a tree.

The word *Tree* is a mental label you place on an event that gives you the illusion of knowledge. As soon as you create the mental label it reduces the possibility of the event showing up as anything other than the label you put on it and traps you in a prison of "knowing." However, being able to observe the part of you that automatically generates the label you place on every event in your life creates a space that leads you to a state of presence or stillness. *Stillness* could be defined as awareness without thought. In aware presence you don't automatically label each event in your life and therefore, everything you see is a mystery.

I suggest you change the labeling of your life events in this way: "We call that a tree," "We call that the sun," "We call you a woman," etc. By shifting your language, you move from being trapped in an *is* world to living in a world of mystery, openness, and possibility.

Einstein acknowledged this by saying that the knowledge we have accumulated so far is insufficient to get us to the next level of awareness.

Growing up, you learn a variety of beliefs from your teachers, family, and direct experience, such as the following: The Earth is round, the Earth is the center of the universe, the Sun is the center of the universe, white people are bad, black people are good, communism is bad, socialism is good, democracy is great, and if you eat meat on Fridays, it is a sin.

What does this all mean to you?

As you evolve and become more conscious, you begin to distinguish your database of beliefs from the part of you that observes those beliefs. This is one of the most important distinctions you want to make in researching your own reality. All the spiritual teachers I have read and heard grapple with this concept of *observer* or *witness*. There is a separation between what you have identified yourself to be, which we call the *I* or *me*, and the *observer* of the *I* or *me*.

How this distinction works in my reality is that when an event occurs in my field of now, I automatically put a label on it based on my past conditioning and then I notice the label I put on that event. As soon as I notice the label, the power it had over *me* is reduced. It is as though a gap is created between the event and the labeling of the event. I also notice that the labels I put on events stir up thoughts, images, and physical and emotional reactions. The major benefit I experience from being able to observe this labeling process is that my physical, emotional, and mental body enters a state of relaxation and calm. Examples of this labeling/relaxation process occur all the time—a cigarette being lighted, traffic jams, flight delays, late people, bad weather, the slaughter of whales, winning business contracts, losing business contracts—the list of events goes on and on.

After a while, you begin to realize that you have been living your life in a state of unconsciousness or, as Eckhart Tolle would say, in a *conditioned conceptual reality*, programmed from birth, which you have unquestioningly believed to be the truth. It is not *the* truth—it is *a* truth. It is one possible interpretation, but it is not the only interpretation.

If you live your life believing that yours is the right interpretation, then you are saying that your reality is correct and everybody else's reality is wrong. This is not a very satisfying strategy to use to play the game of life because your beliefs (i.e., truths) will end up conflicting with other people's beliefs, which creates a state of disharmony for you.

How does this understanding of the *I, me, mind*, etc. affect your ability to be a successful IT presenter? The firewall is created by the *I, me, mind* to protect itself from harm. It views the audience as a threat to its survival, which reduces the quality and effectiveness of your throughput.

It has often been said that most people's number one fear is not death but public speaking. What you often find in presenters is a deep psychological concern for safety and survival. These fears arise out of putting the *I*, the *me*, the *little story of me*, the *ego*, the *mind*, *my database*, *my point of view*, etc. on display in front of other people. Being on display makes one vulnerable to attack, ridicule, embarrassment, and psychological annihilation.

When asked to describe these fears and barriers, one often hears words such as "I will be embarrassed," "I will look stupid," "I will do something weird, strange, or odd," "I will be nervous, anxious, go crazy, or lose control," "I will die (ego)," "I will be uncomfortable," "I will do something unnatural, which will not be me," "I will look unprofessional, inappropriate, and be rejected."

All these thoughts evolve from an underlying unconscious fear that if the *I* lets go of control, if the *I* lets go of its firewall, the *I* will be annihilated. And, in one sense, this is true. The *I* will be annihilated. And yet, as stated in *The Way of Transformation*, "It is only by exposing oneself over and over again to annihilation that the indestructible Being within each person can arise." This is a wonderful quote that was given to me by one of my teachers, Werner Erhard, and I pass it on to you.

When you have the courage to risk being open, authentic, and vulnerable in front of the audience, you are given the key that releases you from the prison of your mind. What is on the other side of those prison walls? What is on the other side of your firewall? There, you'll find the freedom from suppression and the freedom to express yourself fully with power, commitment, and clarity.

In taking this risk you are shifting from a 56k connection to a full-duplex, present-time, broadband connection to the audience. This is the direction to go in order to expand your ability to be an effective presenter in front of an IT audience.

The fear has its origin in what you suspect the audience will think about you when you are talking in front of the group. When you present a piece of data from your internal database, you are presenting a little piece of what you consider yourself to be. You worry, "Does the audience like me or does the audience not like me?" You care about what the audience thinks, which blocks the broadband flow of energy. Every time you speak, you wait for an echo to come back from the audience saying, "We still love you."

This psychological consternation lasts until you eventually say to yourself, "I don't care anymore about what the audience thinks about *me*." When you don't care anymore, you are no longer inhibited by the audience. You are free and move, as George Bernard Shaw said, from being "a feverish, selfish little clog of ailments and grievances complaining that the world will not devote itself to making you happy" to the broadband world of present time, love, and compassion.

The conversation inside your head now begins to shift from you to the purpose of the conversation, which is to be of service and make a contribution to the audience. When this breakthrough occurs, the firewall disappears and you go from a 56k dial-up connection to a broadband connection to the space in the room.

Now, your attention is focused on manifesting your intention in the space of the room. You no longer have to maintain the defenses of the firewall. All your CPU power is on offense, which then maximizes your ability to conduct the conversation in the room effectively.

The vast majority of people, when faced with the prospect of annihilation, never risk entering the arena of public speaking. They spend their entire career just *watching* the show rather than *being* the show. IT professionals cannot retreat to their chairs and watch the show. Their responsibility requires them to stand up and deliver presentations to the customers.

When IT presenters stand in front of the audience, they usually hide behind their firewalls. They are in Data Land and, when they deliver their communication, they are both verbally and physically invisible. The audience then gets to watch an unconscious, uncommitted, invisible data dumper. Anyone wonder why IT presentations are so ineffective?

There is an old joke about IT presentations: "What is the difference between an IT presentation and a funeral?" The answer is: "You know why you're at the funeral."

The psychological blocks and barriers common to IT presenters are unconscious. Unconscious means you are not aware of them or of the fact that they stop the flow of your power and limit your full self-expression. Through training, coaching, and exercises, you can become conscious of the barriers within yourself and release the power of your speaking.

My coaching goal is to free IT presenters from these psychological constraints and help them find the courage to face their fears. The old saying, "Face your fear and the death of fear is certain" makes sense to me.

In my own life, the psychological block that imprisoned me was the fear of rejection. The little voice inside my head said, "Alan, if you really reached out, opened up, and expressed yourself, people would realize that you are just a shy little boy from Bergen County, New Jersey." This thought of exposure kept me trapped in the prison of my mind.

Then one day I was faced with an uncomfortable choice. I could either stay in the hellhole of my suffering or jump into the Zone of Annihilation. I made the choice to jump. And, in that moment, I escaped from the prison of my mind and experienced freedom for the first time in my life. Let me share that story with you.

It was in 1974. I was in a hotel ballroom with about 200 people taking a training course on public speaking and self-expression in San Francisco. Part of the training included standing up and taking a microphone and sharing yourself with the other trainees.

After you shared, people would acknowledge your effort by clapping. A great share, one that "moved the room," would receive a robust applause; a so-so share would receive polite applause. Thus, you got immediate feedback about the quality of your sharing. And, for someone who had never publicly opened up and was concerned about rejection, it couldn't get any more terrifying than this.

The program had been ongoing for six weeks and I hadn't yet shared. It seemed just about everybody except me had shared. I felt an internal pressure to stand up and share myself. I told myself the next time the trainer asked if anyone wanted to share I was going to raise my hand. I remember preparing what I would say and rehearsing it in my head because I certainly didn't want to make a mistake and look like a fool. And then the moment arrived. It was around 10:30 in the morning at the Holiday Inn® on Fisherman's Wharf.

Marcia, the trainer, asked if anybody would like to share. A number of people raised their hands. I didn't. I sat in my chair and listened to the voices inside my head. One voice said, "Raise your hand," and the other voice said, "You are not ready; you don't want to embarrass yourself, especially in front of the women in the room."

Back and forth the voices spoke, one saying "Do it now" and the other saying "Wait." Finally, I thought, "Screw it, just do it," and I raised my hand and took the biggest, scariest leap of faith in my life. I gave up control and the constant attempt to look good.

I knew being suppressed and stewing in my mental cauldron of thoughts was not working. So, leaping into the unknown seemed like the only option to take. I raised my hand and the voices inside my head stopped.

As I raised my hand, Marcia saw me and immediately called my name. In the following two minutes, my experience of living life was forever altered. The microphone was passed to me. I leaped out of my chair and for fifteen seconds in a loud and fast voice I blurted out: "Good morning. My name is Alan Carroll and I have voices inside my head. One voice says to do this and the other voice says don't do this. All I want you to know is it is Saturday morning and I am here. Thank you."

So much for preparation, wanting to move the room and impress the women. The applause was polite. But what was transforming for me was that I experienced something I had never experienced before: I tasted the space of freedom from the suppressive inner voice of my mind. I had let go of wanting to look good and given up the need to be in control. I had risked annihilation. I had risked looking like a fool. I had risked not looking cool and not having my act together. And, in return for this risk, I was given a profound gift, an awareness of my true self, and the experience of my Being, which is beyond the ego. I woke up from a mental dream and became present to the space.

The trainer drew the attention of everyone, then pointed to me and said, "That is what it looks like when you break through."

It was like being in an egg. You don't come out of the egg as an eagle with a twelve-foot wingspan. You come out of the egg a tiny eaglet, very vulnerable and easily injured. By having the courage to give up wanting to look good, I had unknowingly climbed out of the hellhole of my unconscious mind and moved into a more open, lighter, and conscious space. I was no longer concerned about what the audience thought of me. I was willing just to be myself. It was wonderful and continues to this day to be wonderful, just being myself in front of the audience. The unconscious firewalls I had in place to protect myself dissolved and I escaped from a mental prison I hadn't even known I was in.

To be an effective presenter, you must discover the psychological barriers and fears blocking your full self-expression. Find these blocks that stand in the way and, rather than move away from them, move toward them. There is an old Zen saying: "That which stands in the way is the way." For example, if you are afraid of being silly, then do something silly. If you are afraid of looking like a fool, do something you think would be regarded as foolish. Silly and foolish is what you erroneously think the audience will think about you when you act a certain way. Therefore, you don't act out of fear of how you think the audience will respond. You are being controlled by what you think the audience will think about you. You are not free just to be yourself.

Being controlled by how you think the audience will respond makes you a puppet or a doormat. You are being pulled around by the strings and stepped on by the feet of the audience. In chapter four, which is titled "Own the Room," we will address this issue and begin to switch from being dominated to doing the domination. You will learn that by becoming more assertive, the audience, rather than being upset, becomes more respectful and interested in the conversation.

If you have the opportunity to watch yourself on videotape being silly and foolish, you will see it doesn't look nearly as bad as you thought. In fact, it looks like a self-assured human being with power, confidence, and clarity. You'll discover that you were basing your behavior on a mind-created delusion.

Now, let us explore the steps necessary to dismantle the firewalls and the benefits that you will accrue. To maximize the data throughput and increase your effectiveness, you need to create a presentation strategy that gives you access past the firewalls and into the private network of your audience.

The firewall is a psychological entity whose design function is survival. It is put in place by the mind to protect itself from harm. The firewall is analogous to a wall built of bricks. Every time you remove a brick from the wall, you create an opening through which data, communication, and energy can flow. The more bricks you remove, the greater will be your rapport, affinity, and throughput with the audience.

The future is broadband. It would be hard to find anybody who prefers a 56k dial-up connection. Broadband is a source of satisfaction on the Internet and is the source of satisfaction in your presentations.

Broadband means to be yourself without any firewalls between you and the audience. You are no longer inhibited by the audience. You no longer worry about what the audience thinks about you. You have achieved a state of consciousness in which you are open, present, vulnerable, and free from inhibition. You have now regained your power for full self-expression.

How do you dismantle the firewall?

If the firewall is in place to protect the *I, me, ego* from harm, then the presenter needs to create an environment in which all the participants feel safe. I call this environment a *safe space*. In a safe space, the audience feels no psychological need to protect itself. If there were no need for psychological protection, there would be no need for a firewall. And without a firewall, the speaker will be granted access into the private network of the audience.

This concept of a firewall helps explain why IT presentations are usually so ineffective. Without a safe environment, the mind tells the firewall to stay up. When the firewalls stay up, the transfer of data between the presenter and the audience flows through a smaller pipe. The smaller pipe means the connection shrinks down to a 56k level of throughput. The less throughput there is, the lower your effectiveness and your audience's satisfaction will be.

The good news is that there is a simple formula, which, if followed, will grant you access through the firewalls of the audience. All you have to do is focus on removing as many bricks as possible between you and the audience. Bricks are removed through communication. The more communication that is exchanged in the space, the more bricks that are removed. You start the process by removing the bricks inside your reality. You open yourself up. You share yourself. You reach out, shake hands, and get into communication with the space.

Why? Because the audience's firewalls are in place to protect them from harm. By opening yourself up, you are rendering yourself harmless. Once they see that you are open and harmless, it takes away the justification to keep the firewall in place. As it is reduced, the room becomes lighter and the throughput of communication increases.

Working for more than thirty years with hundreds of audiences, large and small, this response has proven itself true every single time. At the start of each presentation, firewalls are at their thickest; at the end of each presentation, firewalls are thinner. The space is lighter, the "Being" is more present, and the flow of communication is greater.

Think of this lighter space like a hot-air balloon. There are two ways to make a hot air balloon go up: put heat into the balloon and release ballast. As you remove bricks from the firewall, you are throwing off ballast and the space gets lighter. The opposite is also true. If you have withheld communication, it adds bricks to the wall and the space gets heavier.

Initially, sharing yourself and removing bricks is an act of courage because you are lowering your defenses and making yourself more vulnerable in front of the audience. But soon, you'll discover that it doesn't take any courage at all. In fact, you'll begin to enjoy the process and look for every opportunity to share yourself, realizing that your ability to contribute and be of service to the audience is directly related to the number of bricks that have been removed from the firewalls in the space.

Another benefit is that, as you increase your vulnerability and openness, it moves you into the space of just being yourself in front of the audience. Often, after training sessions, the IT professionals will admit that they were not being themselves in front of customers. They were playing a role that was not authentic. Now they are relieved to discover that all they need to do is just be themselves in front of the customer. Being yourself makes you a human being and not some data-dumping IT robot. And, when you reveal your humanity, the humanity in the audience will respond. Sharing yourself will differentiate you from other IT professionals who just make love to the data. The sharing and openness need to be deliberate and relevant to the conversation. It is a great way to hold the attention of the audience and establish your credibility.

Another benefit of reducing firewalls is an increase in your effectiveness. Effectiveness can be measured by the amount of information retained by the audience over time.

Being psychologically vulnerable, visible, and open is essential to becoming a powerful and effective speaker. We can draw an analogy from the television show *Star Trek*. The ship on *Star Trek* is called the *Enterprise*. When the *Enterprise* is attacked, Captain Kirk tells the weapons officer to raise the shields. The shields surround the *Enterprise* and prevent the enemy phasers and photon torpedoes from causing damage. But in public speaking, when your shields and firewalls are up the flow of communication between you and the audience is reduced. In order to maximize the flow you need to lower your shields, which psychologically make you vulnerable in the space.

Once again, it takes courage to disarm and open yourself in front of the audience in the beginning. It is so much safer to wrap yourself around your PowerPoint slides, concentrate on the data, and just be a data dumper like everybody else.

Why even risk it? Remember this business saying: *Differentiate or Die.* Do you want to spend your entire career playing the presentation game just like everybody else? Or do you want to be regarded by your customers as an outstanding presenter? Do you want to be of service, make a contribution, and have an impact on the well-being of your customers? If so, begin to explore the space that exists on the other side of the firewall. Each time you risk moving outside your firewall, a little voice sensing danger is going to tell you something terrible is about to happen.

If you are seduced by this message, you will remain trapped in the prison of your mind for the rest of your life. The little voice is not a risk taker and has no interest in you becoming a great presenter. The little voice is your constant companion that labels, judges, assesses, and evaluates every event that occurs in your field of now and even the events that occur in your dreams. As a presenter, you look out at the audience and the little voice will tell you what the audience thinks of you. For those of you who have never heard the little voice, sit down, close your eyes, stop speaking, and just listen for ten seconds. If you still don't hear the little voice, then perhaps what you heard was: "What little voice? I don't hear a little voice inside my head. What is he talking about?" That is the little voice I am talking about inside your head.

As you evolve as a public speaker, you will need to release the suppress button of inhibition and have the courage to step beyond the prison walls of your mind. You will need to have the courage to risk being a fool, to face annihilation, and to have your worst fears exposed in front of the audience.

The dismantling of the firewall is part of the responsibility you have as the manager of the conversation. You cannot and should not expect the audience to take the lead in this process. You have to take action. The following are some communication strategies you can use to create a safe space, lower your shields, and remove bricks from the firewalls in the space.

First, let's start with asking a question: "When does the conversation, the search for common ground, and firewall brick pulling begin?"

Often, the presenter thinks the conversation/presentation starts when he or she is in front of the audience. I suggest starting the conversation as soon as possible. It could start before the day of the presentation or it could start when you walk into the room.

When you start the conversation, you are not only in the data delivery business but also in the building relationships, rapport, and common ground business.

Here are some suggestions of things to do before, during, and after the presentation.

Before the Day of the Presentation

The bricks start being pulled through communication before the audience enters the room. Be in communication with the audience— send them e-mails, regular mail, or give them a telephone call. Let them know the purpose and key points of the conversation and ask them what they would like to have addressed. Provide all the logistical information about start times, room locations, maps, breaks, lunch, contact people, and where to park. Make note of any common ground you have with the participants or they have among themselves.

For example, shared acquaintances, places you have visited, technology background, educational background, books read, movies seen, events attended, sports, vocation, religion, beliefs, history, hobbies, and television shows can all create common ground. Knowing this information ahead of time allows you to introduce it when you meet the people at the presentation. Communication before the presentation starts to shift the expectations of the audience from being unknown to becoming familiar. It gives the participants a greater sense of certainty about what to expect and therefore reduces the *ego/mind* need to maintain a firewall. Communicating in advance sends the message that you care and reflects the level of service your company will provide them in the future when they become a customer.

The Day of the Presentation

The conversation/presentation doesn't start when you walk to the front of the room. It starts when you first walk through the door. The warm-up period is important because it is much easier to do the brick pulling during the informal gathering time than trying to do it from the front of the room.

Here are some possible communication strategies you can employ on the day of the presentation but before the presentation actually starts. Whether you are at your facility or the customer facility, you still are the Manager of the Conversation and the role you play is the one of host or hostess. The participants should be treated with hospitality and as honored guests.

Do you have greeters? Is there someone to welcome the participants and give them directions? Have you put any signage in place that gives clear directions?

When participants walk into the room, greet them. Introduce them to other participants. In this informal time, you have direct access into the other people's private network.

Listen to what they say. The more you know about their world, the better you will be able to shape the conversation to meet their needs. As the leader, you need to take the initiative to meet people. Human beings often seem reluctant to walk up and introduce themselves to the leader.

For your own comfort, shake hands and meet as many people as possible before you go to the front of the room. Shaking hands symbolizes warmth and openness and communicates you have no weapon in your hand. The only time in most business cultures when you can actually touch a stranger physically, male or female, without giving offense is when you shake his or her hand.

Every culture seems to have its own greeting dance. For example, kissing once on one cheek, kissing twice on both cheeks, touching noses, hugging, touching foreheads all expose an intimate connection. For example, when I was in South Africa, the students taught me a local handshake that I used every time I met them. It always put a smile on their faces.

You especially want to meet the people you don't know. Any attack/resistance will most likely come from the person with whom you have the least rapport. Most people's tendency is to walk into the room and go toward someone they know because it feels comfortable. When you introduce yourself to another person, he or she is forced to come out from behind the firewall and open up to you. This communication exchange is a wonderful time to begin exploring other people's worlds.

One of the greatest gifts you can give another human being is to listen to them fully. If you want people to like you, ask them interested questions about themselves. Most people are more focused on themselves than on other people. You can differentiate yourself by being interested in the people in the room.

When first meeting the participants, try to remember their names because it is a great rapport-building tool. If you use people's names, it shows that you care about them. These memory techniques can help you remember names.

- Have it as your intention to remember the person's name.
- Repeat the person's name three times in the first two or three sentences of the introduction.
- Collect business cards. Arrange them on a paper corresponding to the seating pattern in the room. Having the business cards will help you remember the participants. The cards are also useful in accurately entering their information into your database.
- Make nametags or tent cards. On the nametags, make the first name bold so you can easily read it at a distance. The ideal place for the nametag is the upper right part of the chest so you can easily see it when walking up to someone to shake hands. Use people's names during the presentation. This reinforces the relationship, helps you to learn their names, and is one of the many *keep-alives* or *hello packets* that brings the listeners' attention back to the presentation.
- Ask people you know to introduce you to people you do not know. Why? Because the person you know is saying to his or her friend, "This person is a friend of mine." This technique helps to build rapport faster, thus dismantling the firewall more quickly because you are using the leverage of an existing relationship to springboard into the private network of the new person.

There are not only firewalls between you and the audience but also between the participants. You are playing the role of host, so introduce participants to each other. If you know their common ground, tell them, because it provides an excellent starting point for their conversation. This common ground will also be beneficial later on during the presentation because you can use things you heard to help emphasize a point or acknowledge the contribution of a participant.

For example, if you know someone's interest is fishing, you can use fishing analogies to illustrate the conversation. Using information that comes from a participant will make that person feel recognized and valued.

Have music playing. The music you select depends on the type of energy you want to create. You can play relaxing, smooth jazz, classical, up-beat music like classic rock tunes, or popular current hits. You could even play music from the culture in which the presentation is taking place.

Most presenters do not play music, so this differentiates you and makes *your* show a richer experience. Music helps to reduce tension in the audience, which reduces the need to maintain a protective firewall.

Food and drinks are another means to create a comfortable, intimate, and safe atmosphere. The greater the informality, the more disarming it will be. The goal is to create a space that will relax the defenses of the audience.

During the Presentation

Now that the connecting and gathering phase of the conversation is over, the official part of the presentation begins.

How can you massage the space and relax defenses so that the resistance to opening up and communicating is reduced? Facilitate participation as soon as possible. Get the audience to speak in the first three to five minutes. This will be easier if you have pulled a lot of bricks during the connecting and gathering phase.

I call one technique I use to accomplish this *The Level of Expertise*. After you have introduced yourself and stated the purpose of the conversation, say something like this: "Before I move on, I want to get a sense of your experience with the subject of the conversation. How many of you have been involved in it for less than a year? How many for two to three years? Five years or more? For how many is this a brand new subject?"

Ask the people with considerable experience follow-up questions. You can list the years of experience on a flip chart and have someone add up the years of experience the group (including yourself) has on the subject. This becomes the group database. This accomplishes three things: first, it pulls several bricks; second, it lets everybody know where the knowledge lies in the room; finally, it lets you adjust the gradient level of the conversation to meet the level of expertise in the audience.

Share stories and experiences with the audience. A story is a factual or fictional account of an event. Experience is active involvement in a particular activity. I believe that your most valuable content is your stories and experiences about the information you are presenting. If you don't have any stories or experiences, you might have a credibility barrier with the audience. The audience wants certainty that what you are selling actually works. If you have no experience, you are less believable. It is like claiming to be a guide who can take someone from one point to another when you've never been to the final destination.

Another value of sharing stories and experiences is that they promote intimacy in the space. When you make yourself vulnerable, the audience will open up in return. The reason the audience has the firewall up in the first place is to protect and defend themselves from you. You are initially perceived as a threat because you are "not one of us." Sharing stories and experiences makes you more "one of us." It establishes greater common ground upon which to build the relationship.

When the audience sees you as open and vulnerable, they don't need to defend themselves and so don't need a firewall for protection. Stories and experiences are disarming. I would encourage you to share yourself as deeply as possible. Your sharing of self creates a more intimate environment in the room.

Being an authority on the subject matter gives you the confidence to project your energy into the space. The thicker the ice is under your feet, the more power you will have in the room. If you have not earned the right to talk on the subject at hand, you're likely to be hesitant and uncertain in your delivery. Have you taken the time to plan and practice your presentation? Failing to plan is planning to fail.

Ideally, you should know thirty times more about the subject than you will be using in your talk. If you are an authority on the subject matter, you are standing on thick ice. You will be confident in your ability to fire the data across the space and you will have no fear of being asked a question that you cannot answer.

Listen to the audience. Put yourself in their shoes. What are their concerns, cultural background, loyalty to the conversation, and knowledge level? The audience is listening to you through their conditioned reality. The more you understand that reality, the better you will be at navigating past their firewalls and positioning the data in a manner they can accept.

Always allow the audience an opportunity to contribute to the conversation. When someone asks a question, it may be appropriate to let someone else in the audience answer.

Maintain eye contact with one person in the audience when you are delivering your data packets. Only speak when you have a solid virtual private network (VPN) eye contact connection. This automatically pulls you out from behind your firewall and ensures a high level of consciousness. The more conscious you are, the more effective your speaking will be. This is discussed in chapter four in the section on the Point of Focus.

Facilitate a conversation by asking the audience questions. Encourage the audience to participate. Techniques for accomplishing this will be addressed in chapter seven, which deals with The Art of Questioning.

If you are delivering the presentation in English in a foreign country, pick up a few words of the local language and use them in the conversation. Surely, you can learn to say *hello*, *good morning*, and *thank you*. From time to time, ask the audience how they would say a particular word in their language. Refer to popular subjects such as traffic jams, local sporting events, the World Cup. These references create the impression that you are interested in them.

This completes my suggestions about things you can do to reduce firewalls and create rapport, relationships, and common ground during the presentation.

After the Presentation

Here are several ways to continue the brick-pulling process and build a network of relationship with the audience:

- Collect names, addresses, phone numbers, titles, company names, and e-mail addresses and enter them into a database program.
- Use your database to send future newsletters, announcements, and updates to your contacts.
- Thank the participants for their participation and attendance at the presentation.
- Send the participants a summary of the presentation, along with a list of action items.
- Follow up with phone calls to answer any questions and to check on the status of the action items.

This completes my suggestions on how to lower the firewalls before, during, and after your presentations. By increasing your ability to dismantle the firewalls, you will notice the quality of your presentations increases.

3

The Structure of
the Conversation

I don't know what your destiny will be, but one thing I know: the only ones among you who will be really happy are those who have sought and found how to serve.

—ALBERT SCHWEITZER

As an IT professional presenter, you are managing a conversation. I use the word *conversation* rather than *presentation* because the definition of presentation suggests lower effectiveness. Presentation is defined as a way to exhibit, show, and display, whereas conversation implies a two-way flow of communication. People will remember more of what they do and say rather than what they hear.

A well-structured conversation is a critical component of your success as a presenter in the IT world. Currently, there are more than six billion people and most of them would have a difficult time understanding your IT conversation because of its abstractness, complexity, and (sadly) boring delivery.

One of the roles you must inhabit as Manager of the Conversation is that of a translator. Your first job is to plug in to the IT abstract world of complexity, then download content into your database of knowledge, to understand what the content means, and finally, translate and clearly deliver that abstract information to the listening audience. That's easier said than done.

This chapter will show you how to structure your communication, which will increase your ability to be a clear and effective communicator. It is divided into three parts:

- The Introduction
- The Body
- The Conclusion

Communicating my meaning clearly is so important that I want to take the time to define some key words in the Structure of Conversation.

Structure is the arrangement of parts or elements of something complex and/or abstract. A tour guide serves as a useful analogy for structure. Think of yourself as standing in front of the audience, taking them on a tour of your IT subject matter. There is a purpose to the tour and the sites or key points they will see along the way.

Complex means something that is involved, intricate, elaborate, and often difficult.

Abstract means existing as an idea but not having physical or concrete existence. Abstract things may not be easy to analyze or understand. IT conversations can often be distinguished as complex and abstract.

Purpose is the reason for which something is done or for which something exists. Purpose is the aim, intention, and point behind the action taken.

Introduction

The introduction of a presentation contains several important elements, which include purpose, enrollment, key points, trial close, rapport building, credibility, logistics, and the transition to the body. For timing purposes, allow 15 percent of the presentation to be the introduction.

DEVELOPING THE PURPOSE

Clarity of purpose is the number one characteristic of the master communicator, but unfortunately, a statement of purpose is almost always missing in IT presentations.

Why is purpose so important? Because your power and decisions flow from being aligned with your purpose. If you are unclear about the purpose of the conversation, then the choices you make, the projection of your energy into the room, and the communication you create will lack vibrancy, clarity, and effectiveness.

Vibrant means spirited, lively, full of life, energetic, vigorous, vital, animated, sparkling, effervescent, vivacious, dynamic, stimulating, exciting, passionate, fiery, and sometimes feisty.

Purpose is your source of power. It energizes you and illuminates the data. It is much easier to manage the space of the room if you are standing in the light of purpose. However, most presenters are not always clear on the purpose of the conversation because they haven't been trained in the distinction of purpose. They don't realize how important clarity of purpose is to a successful presentation.

Imagine guiding a group of people down a dark tunnel. In one scenario, you are using a powerful flashlight; in the second scenario, you have a tiny candle. Clarity of purpose is like the flashlight; it illuminates the space.

Purpose follows understanding needs. The speaker needs to understand and diagnose the audience's pain to prepare a conversation that will heal the pain. One difficulty the engineer faces is insufficient information about the customer in order to diagnose the problem accurately.

Here's one of the first questions I ask when invited to do a presentation: "What is the audience's need or pain for which my presentation is a solution?" I want to make sure they are hungry for the data food I will serve them.

A presenter, who is often a systems engineer, has an enormous number of product features, functions, and benefits on which to draw. But the engineer needs to know what the specific disease is in order to mix the correct prescription. The prescription is the medication or treatment that will cure the disease or reduce the pain of the customer.

What do I have to give that will be perceived as valuable? What do I have that will make a contribution and be of service to the audience?

The definition of sales is identifying the customer's need/pain and how your features, functions, and benefits will solve it. If you can do that, it increases the probability the customer will buy your solution.

Making a presentation employs the same concept. The speaker has identified the customer's need/pain and has prepared a conversation to address it.

The conversation is not about the ego of the presenter. The ego/ mind gets in the way of a smooth flow of data. The ego/mind is concerned about looking good, not making a mistake, not being embarrassed, and not making a fool of itself.

At a higher level, the presenter is not concerned about looking good; instead, he or she is there to serve the purpose of the conversation—to be of service to the audience.

Consider the story of three stonecutters who were asked what they were doing. The first said he was cutting stones, the second said he was cutting stones to build a wall, and the third said he was cutting stones to build a wall for the mightiest cathedral in the world as a testament to the glory of God.

The same could be asked of you and your presentation. What are you doing? One IT professional says he is delivering data, the second says he is delivering data to help the customer, and the third says she is being of service and contributing to the customer's ability to create solutions that will improve the quality of life on the planet. The last thing the audience wants to see is someone just "doing his or her job," someone who exhibits no passion, excitement, or enthusiasm for what is being done.

Purpose illuminates the conversation. If you are just doing your job, then you have the brightness of a 25-watt lightbulb; however, if you are being driven by a powerful purpose, you will illuminate the room like a 200-watt lightbulb. The greater the illumination is, the greater your charisma. Charisma is a compelling appeal that can inspire devotion in others.

The first step to developing a purpose statement is to understand the audience's needs or pain. What business challenges and problems do they face? How can your solution, functions, and benefits cure their disease?

One way to describe this understanding of the audience's needs is your ability to listen to the "listening" of the audience. The audience is watching and interpreting your presentation through a filter that has been conditioned by their experiences and knowledge.

You want to be able to orchestrate your communication so that the listeners believe that you really understand their world. In other words, listen to the listening of the audience. For example, in writing this book, I am listening to the listening of the reader. The reading audience is IT professionals who want to improve their presentation skills. Every sentence I write is intended to support that listening and every sentence you speak in your presentations should be to support the listening of your audience. By doing this, you will achieve a high level of rapport and credibility and you will keep the audience's attention focused on the presentation. Therefore, the purpose of the conversation is to show how your solution will heal the audience's pain. If you can convince them of that, they will pay attention and move forward in the sales cycle.

If you cannot convince the audience that they have an explicit business pain, don't expect them to give you their full attention, don't expect them to pay the full retail price, and don't expect them to want the solution now.

However, if the audience recognizes that they have explicit needs and their business will experience significant losses without your solution, they will not only pay attention to the conversation, they won't hesitate to buy your medicine at full retail, and they probably wanted your solution yesterday.

From the presenter's perspective, making money is the by-product of serving the audience. If serving occurs, you will achieve your sales call objective and the sales cycle will move forward.

THE BENEFITS OF CLARIFYING THE PURPOSE

There are two main benefits to clarifying the purpose of your conversation with the audience:

1. *Understanding*
   The lack of a clear purpose for the conversation makes it more difficult for the audience to understand it and reduces your effectiveness. Purpose provides the context of the conversation and holds the content. If you do not have a clear context, then it is more difficult for the audience to remember the content.

2. *Choice*
   If there is no clearly stated purpose, the speaker and the audience will have difficulty distinguishing which communications are on message and which ones are off message. This inability to distinguish between them often leads conversations down some rat holes. However, if you understand clearly the purpose of the conversation, then it's easy to determine whether every communication, be it is PowerPoint slides, demonstrations, questions, flip charts, verbal responses, etc., are helpful or not. For example, if the purpose of the conversation has been declared to be the color orange, then when orange appears in the space, it is clearly understood to be on purpose. However, if blue, green, red, yellow, etc. appear in the space, it is clear that these communications are probably off purpose. Purpose becomes the guiding star the presenter uses to create, navigate, and keep the conversation on track.

Let's take the following statement as an example: "The purpose of the presentation today is to expand your understanding of Voice over IP." You would make this statement during the introduction and if you are using PowerPoint slides, you should say it when you show your title slide.

The purpose of this book can serve as another example: "The purpose of this book is to expand your ability to communicate with audiences effectively by developing the skills of self-expression and awareness."

One interesting characteristic of purpose is that it occurs outside of time, whereas the points or objectives in the conversation occur inside of time. For example, if the purpose is to expand the audience's understanding of Voice over IP, you will never achieve it because the possibilities are endless. However, here are three achievable objectives for the conversation: (1) to define Voice over IP, (2) list the three major players in the Voice over IP marketplace, and (3) discuss five hardware components that are necessary in a Voice over IP solution. All these specific points can be measured in time.

Intention is the energy that moves you along your line of purpose. A high-intention person is not distracted from his or her purpose; a low-intention person is easily distracted.

The old truism "You can lead a horse to water but you cannot make it drink" is especially true in presentations. You can provide the water, but the question of whether any participants will drink from the data well will depend on their thirst for the purpose. That is why it is essential to understand the audience's pain and clearly communicate how the purpose will alleviate that pain during your introduction.

This completes the discussion of purpose, so let's move on to expanding your understanding of enrollment.

Enrollment refers to signing on to something of value that you want. For example, let's say you want to participate in an upcoming seminar on Internet Security. You register and your name is placed on the class list. You now have enrolled in the seminar. However, for the purposes of this discussion, I want to use a slightly different definition of enrollment. Enrollment occurs when you see a future possibility and then show that possibility to the audience in present time. The audience in turn sees the value, understands the benefit, and becomes enrolled in that possibility. They now believe that the presentation/conversation has value, will reduce their pain, solve their business problem, and help them achieve their goals.

> **Coaching Tip**
>
> In a PowerPoint presentation, the first slide is often referred to as the *title slide*. You should refer to it as the *purpose slide*. This will naturally lead into your purpose statement.

Enrollment can also be referred to as WIIIFM, which stands for *What is in it for me?* When the audience is sitting in the room and listening to the purpose of the presentation, they are asking themselves, "How does this relate to my world? What is the benefit to me?"

Value for customers usually falls into one of three categories:

- Making money
- Saving money
- Personal

If your business solution will not make or save money for the customer, convincing the CFO to sign on will be more challenging.

Personal benefits could be such intangibles as knowing that your beeper will not go off at 2:00 A.M., that you can leave the office by 5:00 P.M., that you will have more time to spend with your family, or that you will have the largest network infrastructure in New York City.

You should address this WIIIFM question at the beginning of the introduction phase of the presentation because it is the key to enrollment and enrollment is central to holding the audience's attention.

Let's draw an analogy with negotiation: You are demanding that the audience give you their attention during the presentation. The audience will accede to your demand *if* you can provide a rationale. In this case, the rationale is your WIIIFM statement. If you can't answer the WIIIFM question, then you can't complain when the audience doesn't pay attention to your conversation.

In my observation, the typical IT presenter starts with a title slide and then immediately goes to the agenda slide. Very little, if any, enrollment takes place in a typical presentation.

Coaching Tip

In a PowerPoint presentation, the second slide is usually the *agenda slide*. I suggest making the second slide the *enrollment/ WIIIFM slide*. The WIIIFM slide tells them why they should pay attention to you. It is directly related to the challenges and needs of their business.

The following is a simple example of a purpose statement followed by enrollment: "The purpose of today's conversation is to expand your understanding of the importance of Voice over IP. Now why should you take the next forty-five minutes of your time to focus on this conversation? Two weeks ago, when we met, you said your number one concern was to increase your profitability and one way of doing this was by reducing your costs. The Voice over IP solution is a proven technology that will reduce your costs and thus increase your profitability. Here are the three key points I want to address today: One, what is Voice over IP? Two, how can VoIP be easily implemented into your organization? And three, what is the projected cost savings? If we can address these three areas to your satisfaction, the next step I propose is to invite you and your technical support team to our demonstration center to show you how a VoIP solution would work within your organization. How does that sound to you?"

> **Coaching Tip**
>
> Every presentation you do is an enrollment event. You are always enrolling the audience in something, whether it is signing the purchase order, agreeing to another meeting, doing a demonstration, or flying to corporate headquarters.

Now let's shift from the enrollment distinction into the *key points* distinction. How do you decide on which key points to use?

I suggest you imagine yourself standing in front of the audience and ask yourself some important questions:

- What are the needs of this audience?
- What is the purpose of the conversation?

- What is the level of expertise?
- What is the sales call objective?
- Now that I understand these things, what is the greatest contribution I can make to the audience over the next forty-five minutes?
- What is the most value I can give them?
- When they walk away at the end of the forty-five minutes, what key points do I want them to remember?

Choose the key points to include in the presentation based on the answers to these questions.

How many key points should you use? This is an important question because IT presenters often make the error of saturating the space with data, thinking that quantity of data is more important than quality.

You must be concerned about the amount of data you put into the space because every time you communicate a distinction or technical concept, you have the responsibility to make sure the audience clearly understands it.

IT professionals generally do an excellent job in mastering an understanding of the data, but unfortunately, almost all them that I have seen over the last twenty-five years have had little, if any, concern for clarity. It is not their intention that

> ## Coaching Tip
> The power of the WIIIFM statement is directly related to your understanding of the customer's business. The customer is sensitive to your credibility. Do you understand my world? Corporations often hire individuals from a particular business sector and then put them on the team selling into that sector because they have high credibility with the audience.

the audience understand the data. This may seem a bold statement, but it is true.

The ordinary IT presenter often defaults to Data Land and withdraws from establishing a present-time connection to the audience. Without a present-time connection, you can only hope that the audience is going to understand what you are saying because the ability to clarify distinctions to the audience can only occur in present time. You have to be present to know if the audience has clearly understood you.

To minimize the amount of data you dump into the space, limit yourself to no more than seven key points per hour of presentation time. However, you do need to be flexible because this can vary depending on the level of expertise of the audience and the complexity of the distinctions.

This completes the section on key points, so let's move on to the next part of the introduction, which is called the *trial close*. Normally, at the end of the presentation, you make a request for the customer to take some action. This action could be agreeing to buy the solution, schedule a demonstration, schedule another meeting, attend a seminar, or meet with a senior executive. In sales, this request is called a close or what I refer to as a *call for action*. If there is no action or commitment in response to the presentation, then sales management (the ones who are paying for the call) would have to question its value.

During the introduction, there is the opportunity for a trial close, in which you plant the seed of future action on the customer's part. For example, you could say, "The purpose of today's conversation is to expand your understanding of some of the latest developments in network security. This is important because last week you told us that over the past several months your network has been attacked and valuable data has been compromised."

The trial close in this instance could be something like ". . . and, if we can show you to your satisfaction how our solution will solve your security concerns, then I propose you move ahead with the implementation of our solution. Does this sound reasonable to you?"

If they say *yes*, then the rest of the presentation, showing your security solution, leads up to asking for the order in the conclusion.

If they say *no*, ask what prevents them from agreeing to your request. As you get better at playing the sales game and build rapport with the client, the public request for action may have been already agreed to in private so that there are no surprises.

The next part of the introduction should continue building rapport, common ground, and relationships. Throughout the sales cycle, which includes the presentation, you are always looking to build rapport, common ground, and relationships with the customer.

There are a number of standard questions related to sales: *When do you close?* Answer: *Always be closing.* Question: *When do you build rapport?* Answer: *Always be building rapport.*

The steps for building rapport were addressed in chapter two, "Through the Firewall and Beyond."

Here are some techniques to employ at the beginning of your presentation:

1. Thank the audience for the opportunity to address them.
2. Meet and interact with as many people as you can before the formal part of your presentation.
3. Start your talk by looking at the people who are smiling and are on your side.
4. Memorize the first sentence or two in the introduction.
5. Never start your talk with an apology.
6. If appropriate, include a zinger, which is something that arouses curiosity. It could be a startling fact, a story, a striking

question, a cartoon on a PowerPoint slide, or a joke. Whatever the zinger is, it should be related to the purpose of the conversation and it should be something that you are sure will have the desired effect.

Logistics can be another part of the introduction. This includes the management, handling, coordination, and execution of the conversation/presentation. Most IT presenters have little awareness on the importance of logistics in the space.

In your role as the host, what does the audience/your guests need to know in order for them to be comfortable and to maintain the integrity in the space? *Integrity* means to be whole and complete. Imagine a vessel that holds water. If you punch a hole in the vessel, the water will flow out. The more holes you punch, the faster you lose the water. The water represents the power of the conversation. If there are a lot of things punching holes in the space, then it weakens the conversation. Integrity in the space can be the physical integrity, as well as more subtle forms of integrity like time and re-creating other people's communication.

The following logistics issues can influence the integrity in the space:

- Cell phones and laptops can disturb the flow of the conversation. Therefore, at the beginning of the presentation, state how you want laptops and cell phones handled in the space. You can simply ask them to turn their cell phones off and close their laptops. At one company in Singapore, management had everyone place their cell phones in a box at the beginning of presentations because they caused such a disturbance. During presentations, I have walked around and physically closed laptops that were open. In my role as the referee, I have given people who kept receiving calls the choice of turning their phones off or leaving the room permanently. It reached a point where I wouldn't tolerate the constant disruption because it was damaging the integrity of the space and affecting the quality of the conversation.

- As the manager of the conversation, you also want to maintain the time integrity. Does the meeting start on time? Does it end on time? When you announce a break, do you end the break on time? One company hired a consulting firm to identify critical success factors to empower the organization. After several months of research, they discovered one key success factor: starting the meetings on time.

- Physical integrity also includes making sure the environment is safe. Are electrical cords taped to the floor so no one trips over them? Are the window blinds down so people are not distracted from the presentation? Is the door closed so people can't look into the room? Is the room well lighted?

- Is the room clean? Have you packed away all the extra stuff that accumulates over time in presentation rooms? Think of it like cleaning your house before inviting friends over. Ideally, you only want things in the space that are needed for the presentation. For example, if you are expecting ten people, have only ten chairs. Put the extra chairs somewhere outside the room. Often, there is a clutter of extension cords, computer wires, power strips, pens, markers, and old handouts from previous presentations in the room. Put everything away. Are the wastebaskets empty? Do all the lightbulbs work? Does the media equipment work? Are the tabletops cleaned? Are your presentation materials neatly prepared? Are the whiteboards erased? If you lay out your presentation materials beforehand, do it neatly as if you are setting a table for an elegant dinner.

When people walk into a space that you have taken the time to prepare so carefully, they will be dazzled.

This completes the discussion of logistics, so let us move on to *credibility*. Credibility is the state of being trusted and believed. Always establish your credibility. How have you earned the right to speak on the subject? If someone is to introduce you, give him or her a 3×5 note card listing all the things you want the audience to know about you. It should ensure that those things will be said. The introduction can create and shape the listening of the audience.

For example, an introduction like this creates a negative listening: "Today, we couldn't have our first choice of speaker, but at the last minute we were able to get Bob. He was not doing anything else and, although he is not as knowledgeable as we would like, I am sure he will do okay. Please welcome Rob . . . er, excuse me, please welcome Bob."

This is an exaggeration, but it highlights the importance of a good introduction. Here is an introduction that creates positive listening from the audience: "Today, we are very fortunate to have Dr. Robert Johnson, the world-famous author of the best-selling book *Voice Over IP*. Dr. Johnson has won numerous awards and holds the chair in physics at both Cambridge and Yale universities. Dr. Johnson is a senior member of the United Nations International Committee on the Development of the Internet in the Third World and it is a great honor to have him with us today. Please welcome Dr. Robert Johnson."

Try to understand the audience's perspective. Are they *for* the conversation or *against* it? Do they have loyalty to another competitor? What is their knowledge of the subject matter? The more you understand the listening of the audience, the better you will be able to shape your presentation to match that listening and gain rapport.

The final part of the introduction is the *transition statement*, which connects the introduction to the body of the talk. One of the key characteristics of master presenters is that they have great transitions in their conversations. The audience never wonders where they are or where they're going because the presenter is guiding them step by step.

Think of yourself as a tour guide, explaining the route of the tour and the key sites along the way. The members of the group always know exactly where they are on the tour. In a well-structured presentation, the audience always knows exactly where they are in the conversation because the speaker makes clear transitional statements.

The Body

A transitional statement from the introduction to the body might sound something like these: "This completes the introduction, so let's move into the main points of the presentation," or "As I mentioned before, the first point is . . ."

You are now into the body of the presentation. Generally speaking, the body comprises about 75 percent of the presentation time. Therefore, if the whole presentation is an hour in length, the body would be approximately forty-five minutes long.

In the introduction, you told the audience what you were going to present. In the body, you develop each of your key points or distinctions.

PowerPoint slides are traditional tools of presentation. However, in addition to PowerPoint slides, you should consider additional tools that can differentiate you from the competition.

For each major distinction, have a mass demonstration and an analogy ready to deliver. Demos and analogies communicate to the audience that you care that they understand the information in the presentation. Why? Because you are taking the time to encapsulate the data to help them assimilate it.

In addition to PowerPoint slides, use the flip chart and the whiteboard if appropriate. Varying the media used helps the audience refocus their attention on the presentation.

After you have developed each point, let the audience know that you have completed this point and are going to move to the next one.

The final component of the body could be a question and answer (Q&A) session. Usually, the presenter conducts this session at the end of the conclusion; however, it is more effective to do so at the end of the body for several reasons:

- You want the last thing the audience hears to be your conclusion, key point summary, purpose, and call for action. If you do the Q&A at the end of the conclusion, then the last thing they hear will be the answer to the last question.
- You manage the timing of the presentation. You know the length of your conclusion, so you can adjust the Q&A session to fit into the time remaining.
- In some situations, when the audience hears the presenter say, "And now I would like to open it up for your questions," some people may leave the room, which affects the integrity of the space.

Introduce the Q&A session by saying something like this: "This completes my final point, but before I conclude, I would like to open it up for your questions." You might also include a test of the audience's understanding by saying, "This completes my final point, but before I conclude, I would like to open it up for your questions. But before I do *that*, let me ask *you* some questions."

If you choose to conduct a test for understanding, then the questions you ask must be low-gradient ones related to the key points in the presentation. You don't want to ask a question that can't be answered.

A simple test reviews the basic points, causes the audience to focus their attention, and stimulates the flow of communication.

TIPS FOR Q&A

Conduct the Q&A session from the *power point position*—the place that is the optimum focal point for the audience. Keep your hand up as you scan the audience for questions because this is the universal non-verbal signal for asking a question. Rephrase and embellish each question, as appropriate, to the entire audience for clarification.

The Conclusion

This completes the section on the body, so we can move on to a discussion of the conclusion, which takes about 10 percent of the presentation time. In the conclusion, you begin by restating the purpose of the conversation, touch on the WIIIFM, state the key points, and end with your call for action, which you mentioned first as your trial close during the introduction. The call for action varies depending on the purpose of the presentation. In a sales situation, your call for action is the commitment you want from the customer to advance to the next stage of the sales cycle. In an internal technical presentation, your call for action might be as simple as asking audience members to send you an e-mail if they have any follow-up questions.

We now have reached the end of the presentation. You should thank your audience for their participation and time. You can acknowledge them by saying, "I enjoyed the opportunity of meeting with you and I look forward to seeing you again." You should also emphasize that you will stay afterward to answer any additional questions. This is important because some people may have been reluctant to speak during the formal part of the presentation. Staying in the room after the presentation also provides another opportunity to establish rapport and common ground. If people in the audience invite you to go out afterward to socialize, accompany them because this is an excellent way to deepen the relationship.

Finally, in order to avoid getting too deep in the technical data, you can announce in the introduction that you have prepared an in-depth handout, which will be available at the end of the presentation. This technique allows you to focus on the key points, avoids over-saturating the space with data, and gives you an "out" when asked a technical question by just referring the questioner to the handout at the end.

To conclude "The Structure of the Conversation," I suggest including the following things in the introduction, the body, and the conclusion of your presentation.

> **Coaching Tip**
>
> How do you manage handouts? If you use handouts, you do not want people reading them while you are presenting. Giving the audience copies of the slides as a handout should be done at the end of the conclusion. However, there are situations where it is appropriate to give the slides out at the beginning, such as if you want them to have a copy to record their notes.

The Structure of a PowerPoint-Based Presentation

PLANNING AND PREPARATION

- Plan your presentation in advance.
- Characterize your audience: technical, non-tech, managerial, or mixed?
- Get clear on your purpose. Address WIIIFM and the key points you want to address.
- What commitment do you want the audience to make?
- What results do you intend to achieve?
- For each section:
    - What PowerPoint images will you use?
    - What mass or analogies will you use?
    - What whiteboard information or flip charts will you use?
    - What are your interaction questions?
- Title Slide—Project and leave up while waiting for the meeting to start.

INTRODUCTION (15 PERCENT OF THE PRESENTATION TIME)

- Purpose Slide—Leave up during the introduction. Build rapport, common ground, and relationships (e.g., "Hi John, great to see you again.").
    - Declare the purpose of the conversation. Develop the WIIIFM by addressing the audience's pain/problem. Seek the audience's enrollment into the presentation by letting them know why they should listen to you. How did you get enrolled in the topic? Share a story or relate an experience.

- Cover any rules of engagement or logistical issues that need to be addressed, such as when to ask questions, and the use of laptops or mobile phones.
- Agenda Slide—Tell them what you're going to cover today with a bullet for each section.
- Agenda Slide—Show it again, highlighting section 1, and then transition to the body of the presentation.

BODY (75 PERCENT OF THE PRESENTATION TIME)

- Section 1, slide 1—Develop and discuss.
  - Use slides, whiteboard, flip charts, mass, analogies.
- Agenda Slide—Highlight next section, transition to next section.
- Section 2 (etc.), Slide 1—Develop and discuss.
  - Use slides, whiteboard, flip charts, mass, analogies.
- Q&A session—If you have a Q&A session, put it here, before the conclusion (never after the conclusion).
  - Transition statement connecting the end of the body to the beginning of the conclusion.

CONCLUSION (10 PERCENT OF THE PRESENTATION TIME)

- Agenda Slide—Highlight the summary—Leave slide up while you summarize.
  - Restate the purpose or the context of the conversation.
  - Restate the enrollment/WIIIFM/pain of the audience.
  - Restate the topics you have covered.
- Close with your call for action.

4

Own the Room

The role you play in front of the audience is that of the leader of the conversation. You are the alpha dog. The audience wants you to express yourself with confidence, assertiveness, commitment, and clarity. No one wants to sit through an hour-long presentation watching an uncommitted, uninspired beta dog perform. However, very few IT professionals own the room. This chapter discusses two ideas: the concept of *owning the room*, which builds on Roger Ailes's idea of *controlling the atmosphere*, and the concept of *strengthening your alpha dog state of mind*. Let's first explore what's meant by *controlling the atmosphere*, as found in Roger Ailes's book, *You Are the Message*.

Control of the Atmosphere

The basic component of controlling the atmosphere is the ability to control time in the space. I have great respect for how IT professionals learn to master detailed technical concepts; if they could learn to control their use of time, they would have the one key ingredient that would make them master presenters. However, when you watch most IT professionals make presentations, it is obvious they are unable to pace their presentation for maximum impact. They have little awareness of the value of pauses because they are focused only on the data.

The *space* Ailes refers to in his book is the physical room and all the objects in the room. Rather than control the space, many IT professionals seem intimidated by it. They are reluctant to move around the room and to use objects, i.e., mass, to help make their points. Everything in the space, including PowerPoint slides, whiteboards, flip charts, and even the people themselves are resources you can employ to reinforce your words. An alpha dog doesn't hesitate to use every tool in the space.

Control of the atmosphere means control of the time and space in which you work. When you control the atmosphere, you're not operating on other people's time. When you own the room, you are not concerned about what the audience may think of you. It is your show. You are free to take your time to express yourself clearly. You do not feel pressure to rush. You do not operate on other people's time.

YOU HAVE NO FEAR OF SILENCE

Presenters who are uncomfortable with silence will try to fill the space with data. Why do presenters interpret silence as uncomfortable?

Because they worry that the audience will think they have lost their train of thought, which would be embarrassing. So, they talk nonstop throughout the presentation and end up looking foolish and unprofessional. A true professional uses silence to gather his or her thoughts and allows the audience to think about what was just said.

YOU USE GESTURES AND MOVE EFFECTIVELY AND ASSERTIVELY, WHEN AND HOW YOU PLEASE

A common problem for IT presenters is the quality of their hand gestures, which I refer to as video, and the movement of their bodies around the room. A presenter needs to be in present time when delivering the conversation. When you are in present time, you have control of your body, so your gestures will be sharp and clear. I call this quality *high definition*. You will rarely see IT presenters come close to creating high-definition video images with their hands. And, because they do not control time, any video image they do create will not be held long enough for the audience to see it clearly. A good high-definition gesture needs be held for at least one full second.

A good way to tell whether you own the room is how you move your body in the space. By observing a presenter's body movements, an audience can determine within seconds if that person is afraid or confident. The presenter need not say a word because body movements reveal his or her inner state. For example, if a senior executive at a major IT company runs to the front of the audience, he is displaying self-assurance, confidence, and an attitude that says "I can't wait to talk with you." In contrast, I have seen IT presenters walk slowly to the front of the room, make no eye contact, and then take a step back from the audience. These are beta dog movements that suggest fear and discomfort. The audience, sensing weakness, may be more likely to go on the attack.

When a presenter's awareness is not in his or her body, the presenter is usually in another world called Data Land. The only time the presenter can regain control over his or her body is during a space packet—the pause between communication packets. You create a space packet by being able to stop speaking. When you stop speaking, you disconnect from Data Land and shift your awareness back into your physical body, a process I call a *body check*. During the body check, you can relax and make sure your feet are grounded. *Grounded* is an electrical term used here as a metaphor for being anchored or connected to the floor of the room. The flow of energy through you is now grounded. An IT presenter in Data Land is not grounded. During the pause, when the presenter consciously reconnects to his or her body, the quality of delivery immediately improves and the presenter takes control of the presentation. The body is the most powerful tool a presenter has to stay in present time and maintain a broadband connection to the audience.

Roger Ailes uses the word *assertive* to describe the body's movement. To be assertive means to be confident, bold, and decisive. These are the characteristics of a leader who's in control of the atmosphere. Either your body moves with purpose or your body moves without purpose. Because most IT presenters are not aware of their bodies, all you see is purposeless movement, which creates a distraction I call *visual noise*. Just as there is auditory noise such as *ums*, *ahs*, and *okays*, there is visual noise, which includes actions such as pacing, hand holding, bending the arm at the elbow, side slapping, fidgeting with objects, etc. All visual noise is unconscious and loudly communicates to the audience that you are a beta dog who is not in control. When you become present, all the visual and auditory noise disappears and the audience perceives you as a polished and professional presenter who owns the room.

YOU MODULATE YOUR VOICE WITH PURPOSE

The old expression "No one will follow an uncertain trumpet" still holds true today. When you stand in front of the audience, you are the trumpet. Either you speak with confidence and certainty or you don't. When you own the room, the quality of your voice reveals your inner state. The audience will form an immediate impression of you from the sound of your voice. Is your voice dull, tight, nervous, monotonous, or harsh, or is it full and melodious? By controlling your voice, you can increase the impact of your delivery. In chapter one, I discussed how to develop the ability to control your voice. Sandy Linver, in her book *Speak Easy,* describes the importance of voice quality: "Slurred, sloppy articulation often reflects jumbled thoughts, vague ideas, or indifference toward your subject or audience, and often accompanies other lazy habits such as sloppy posture."

Use your voice and eyes as you would a rifle. Get ready, aim, and fire your words. The number one tool to increase your power as a speaker is *Point of Focus.* Before you speak, connect to someone's eyes. Once you have made this connection (which I refer to as a VPN or port connection), you download your communication packets. Holding eye contact while talking anchors you, shows confidence, and keeps you in present time. For a complete discussion of the Point of Focus tool, see chapter six.

You can express a range of emotions, including amusement, excitement, and even anger where appropriate. The voice is like a musical instrument, but most presenters just play one monotonous note. When you own the room, you vary the tones of your voice. You make yourself vocally and physically alive to the audience. You are not afraid to be seen.

The ability to convey enthusiasm in front of an audience is one of the most valuable skills a presenter can master, but most IT presenters are very weak in this respect. However, the leader or alpha dog will have mastered this technique. Roger Ailes has two short quotes on energy that I enjoy: "If you have no energy, you have no audience" and "An ounce of energy is worth a pound of technique."

Why is passion or enthusiasm so difficult to express in front of the audience? The reason goes back to the purpose of the mind, which is survival. When you are passionate, you are visible, open, and vulnerable. If you say to your mind, *we are going to be visible, open, and vulnerable*, the mind will respond by saying *no*. Therefore, being enthusiastic in front of the audience is not only courageous but can be contagious.

How do you generate enthusiasm? First, you have to create excitement. Excitement is something that has form to it. You can put on excitement. You can fake excitement. You can make up excitement. You can pretend excitement. As a presenter, you need the ability to get excited. Don't be concerned about enthusiasm—first, you have to generate excitement. Excitement is the outward expression of enthusiasm and inspiration. The purpose of dealing with excitement is to gain enthusiasm. You don't have to pretend enthusiasm. You are already enthusiastic. All you need to do is discover that fact.

Try this exercise designed to break you through to your natural enthusiasm. Over the next seven days, be ten times more excited than you have ever been before in your life. Remember—even if you don't experience it, fake it.

You can practice all over the place. Energy is the ingredient necessary to produce excitement. Get your energy up! When you do that, you can create excitement at any time and the excitement will be appropriate to your enthusiasm.

People are persuaded more by the depth of your conviction than the height of your logic, more by your enthusiasm than any proof you can offer.

—DALE CARNEGIE

In the presentation, your energy level can vary from low tone to a high tone. High tone would be exhilaration and low tone would be death-like. Your energy should be appropriate to the audience. If the audience is at a level 3, you should be at a level 4 or 5. If your energy is too high, the audience will feel uncomfortable and raise their firewalls.

Now let's explore some techniques and moves that will develop your ability to look like an alpha dog at the front of the room.

- Being an alpha dog or leader means that you are psychologically free from being suppressed by the audience. You have no need to operate from behind a firewall. You believe you have a valuable contribution to make to the audience.
- Although the alpha dog dominates the pack, avoid doing anything that would be perceived as dominating the audience because that may offend them. If the audience is offended, it reduces rapport.
- When you talk, make sure you have a solid connection with the eyes of someone in the audience. Only talk after you have given yourself a conscious command to lock on to a person's eyes.
- Don't talk when looking at the empty space between the eyes of the audience.
- Minimize the time you have your back facing the audience while using your PowerPoint slides, whiteboard, or flip chart.
- After you have delivered your communication to a person in the audience, hold eye contact for just a second to make sure your communication has been received.
- When you enter the room and walk up in front of the audience, pause for a second, look at the audience, and feel your feet connected to the floor.

- Stay connected to your feet. Even when you are delivering your data, you should still feel your feet on the floor.
- At the beginning of the presentation, stand in the focal point of the room and keep your feet still. The focal point is centered in front of the audience and an equal distance from each side of the room. Stand up straight and maintain a relaxed yet powerful posture.
- When you transition from your introduction to your first point in the presentation, move from the focal point to another spot on the floor.
- If the customer is behind a table, touch the table with your hand from time to time. This has several benefits: (a) it steadies your body, (b) it shows you are not intimidated, and (c) it puts your scent in the other person's territory so to speak. Unbeknownst to the listener, you are claiming his or her territory as your own.
- When talking to a person in the audience, stand with your body fully facing that person rather than at an angle. To use a naval analogy, it is harder for a submarine to hit the bow of the ship with a torpedo than to hit the broadside of the ship. Angling your body says you are timid and having your body facing the audience fully says you are bold.
- While talking to someone sitting behind a table, walk close to the table and lean your leg against it. You will derive the same benefits as leaning your hand on the table and it is even less noticeable.
- Imagine you are an artist and the room is your canvas. Move your body all over the canvas. Go to the sides, go to the back, and go up the middle. This shows you are free to use the whole space of the room.

- Touch things in the room. This includes walls, flip charts, and even people. Touching things grounds you and spreads your scent around the room. Touching should be done in such a way that the audience is not aware of what you are doing.
- Require the audience to perform for you. For example, throw a tennis ball to someone in the audience and have him or her catch it, pick someone for your demonstrations, ask people questions, make someone the timekeeper, have another check to see if lunch has arrived, etc.
- Change your stance by sitting on the table, sitting in a chair, or leaning down.
- Change the speed at which you move around the room. Most people move their bodies at the same speed and never get out of first gear. Once in a while, you should speed up to second gear.
- Use your whole body, especially your shoulders, arms, and hands, to create gestures and video images. Be bold, visible, and physically committed to the video gestures.
- Throw your voice and body into your self-expression. By doing this, you are committing to the data. Audiences rarely get to see presenters who commit their full self-expression to the data. When you own the room, you are fully expressing yourself. The audience will think "Wow! This data must be important if he's committing his voice and body to it."
- Your own assessment of your actions in front of the room is irrelevant. You are not presenting for yourself—you are doing it for the audience. If the audience likes the way you deliver the message, then do it that way, regardless of what the little voice inside your head may say.

- Try these suggestions to increase the energy in the room:
    - Play lively music (you can have it on your laptop).
    - Have people stand up to stretch.
    - Schedule a break.
    - Lead the audience in taking a deep breath from time to time.
    - Do energy exercises like a powerful karate chop.
    - Sing songs that require body movement.
    - Do physical exercises in the morning like calisthenics.
    - Keep your energy level vibrant via voice and body movements.
    - Include the audience in your demonstrations.
    - In our workshops, at the end of each module, we all stand, kick our right knee in the air, clap our hands together, and yell, "This section of the workshop is history!"
- Sound effects add to your conversation and make you more enjoyable for the audience. Examples of sound effects include snapping fingers, striking the table with your hand, whistling, tapping the side of a glass, clapping, stamping your foot on the floor, crinkling paper and throwing it away, tearing flip charts off the wall, slapping the walls, knocking over the flip chart, adding sound to the PowerPoint slides, etc.
- Your writing on the flip charts should be big and bold. This indicates you are not afraid to be seen. Too often, writing is so small that it is hard to read.
- As the leader of the conversation, you must command the attention of the audience. Think of yourself as a shepherd whose job is to keep the flock of sheep together. The best way to hold attention is to convince the audience of the value of the presentation to their business and remind them of WIIIFM (what is in it for me). The second way to hold attention is to

use *keep-alives*. A keep-alive is a packet sent by one network device to another to verify that it is connected to the network. In the context of a presentation, the presenter is the source router and the people in the audience are the destination router. Therefore, the presenter is not only sending communication packets during the conversation, he is also sending keep-alives. Here are some examples of keep-alives:

- Using a person's name from time to time in the conversation.
- Moving your body toward someone.
- Varying the tone of your voice.
- Connecting with the eyes of someone in the audience.
- Creating silence in the room.
- Getting someone to speak.
- Introducing sound effects.
- Doing something dramatic, such as throwing something over your shoulder but not looking at where it lands, or pouring water on the floor.
- Tossing something at a person who can catch it.
- Doing demonstrations with objects and people.
- Moving to the sides and to the back of the room.
- Having the audience stand up and stretch.
- Touching people.

- The leader of the conversation not only speaks clearly but has developed the skill of listening. Listening can be broken down into two components: creating space to allow the other person's communication to exist and re-creating the other person's communication. Let's look at each of these two areas. What does it mean to create space? When another person speaks, they are placing their thoughts into the public domain. Thoughts coming from their private domain are offered to people in the public space. When these thoughts are expressed, they are judged by the audience as to whether they are right or wrong. The alpha dog has the confidence to set aside judgments. You are now able to hear the other person clearly. Once you can hear the other person, you can re-create that person's communication. *Re-create* means to demonstrate to the person that you got their communication. In re-creation, you use words, tones, physiology, and sometimes mass. Most people are weak at listening because they are unable to put aside their opinions and beliefs. Therefore, they don't fully understand the other person. One of the greatest gifts you can give another person is to listen to and then re-create what was said. Most people are just too busy in their own worlds to take the time to listen.

- The leader of the conversation practices the skill of mindfulness, the art of being fully present in each moment of now. Too often, I see presenters trying to multi-task, such as looking at someone and talking while they reach for a physical object in order to create a demonstration. Mindfulness means *not* multi-tasking. You should only reach for the object. Once you have the object, present it to the person. Once the demonstration is complete, put the object down. Practicing mindfulness shows the audience that you are not intimidated and that you are operating the conversation on your time.

- Take a deep breath from time to time and keep your body relaxed. Sandy Linver explains, "Focusing on your own breathing is the most effective method I know for staying in the here and now. Breathing is an essential, central rhythm of your body, so focusing on your breathing means getting back in touch with yourself."

- Introduce and shake hands with as many people as you can. This shows that you are the host of the conversation and the room belongs to you.
- Share personal stories and experiences that are relevant to the conversation. Opening yourself to the audience shows that you are confident and are unafraid to be seen. This attribute can be described this way:

> No one can be loved . . .
> Until they can let themselves be seen.
> No one can be seen . . .
> Until they can learn to love themselves.

- The leader of the conversation is able to stay on point and avoid being sidelined or distracted by people's comments or questions.

In conclusion, owning the room—being the alpha dog—is essential to delivering high-quality IT presentations. It is your show. If you develop this sense of ownership, your audience will look on you as a leader who commands attention and respect.

5

Managing
Resistance

Outwitted
They drew a circle that shut me out,
A heretic, a rebel, a thing to flout.
But love and I had the wit to win,
We drew a circle and took them in.

—EDWIN MARKHAM

Resistance occurs when another person's communication packets are directed toward you and you are unable to accept those communication packets in your space. For example, the customer says,

"I am no longer interested in this piece of crap you call a solution." This is an emotionally charged packet of data directed toward you.

Based on your conditioning, you interpret what that packet of data, tone of voice, and body movement means. Therefore, you could say that the problem is not what happens; the problem is your interpretation of what happens.

It is that interpretation that doesn't give space to the other person's communication because it is a threat to the survival of what you consider to be the truth. *Your truth* is based upon the accumulation of all your experiences stored in your internal database from the first day of your life to the present time. *The other person's truth*, which you are resisting, is the accumulation of data and experiences he or she has stored from birth to the present time.

Both of you are living in a conditioned, conceptualized reality that is disconnected from the real world. In your delusion, you believe your interpretation of the world is true, just as for thousands of years people believed that the earth was flat. You don't live in the real world—you live in a fantasy world constructed by the mind-made self.

When an exterior event occurs in your *field of now*, both parties automatically label that event and give it meaning. Once you have established this meaning, then your behavior automatically correlates to that interpretation.

For example, when a communication packet of data arrives into your space from an outside source, you immediately compare it to what you know to be true. If it doesn't agree, you resist it because it is a threat to your database of thoughts. For example, when Galileo stated that the earth revolved around the sun, that represented a threat to society's database of thoughts, which said the sun revolved around the earth.

When resisting, you have no space to allow this piece of external data that you don't agree with to exist in your field of awareness. You resist it because you experience the other person's communication as a threat to your well-being. You are constantly on the alert to being right and avoiding being wrong. If your mind-made self is challenged, it will automatically react by defending itself, which often includes trying to diminish the sense of self of the person who attacked you. It is an enormous insult to the mind-made self to be seen as wrong.

In resistance, the customer has said something that has diminished your sense of self and you want to attack the other person because obviously he or she is wrong and you are right. However, by understanding the source of resistance, you will be able to begin to transcend the right/wrong game. The essence of this transformation is observing your mental and emotional reactions when someone makes you wrong.

There is nothing else to do. If you can just create a little space between the reaction you are having to the exterior event and the part of you that is observing that reaction, then the tension and resistance will melt away. In its place will be humor, love, and the increased ability to resolve whatever event is presented to you.

Love is giving something the space to be what it is and what it isn't. By allowing another person's communication to exist in your space, you are giving space or love to that person.

More importantly, you are not only giving the other person space, you are giving yourself room to accept your own mental and emotional reactions. The giving of space is an act of love and compassion.

Compassion can be defined as sympathetic understanding of another person's pain. By allowing another person's communication to exist, you are in the space of compassion.

Resistance is the exact opposite of compassion. Resistance is the absence of love. You have no space for that communication packet to exist in your world.

You will not be successful in managing resistance if you do not allow the customer's packet of communication to exist in your world. You need to reach a point where anyone can say anything to you and it just rolls off of you like water rolls off a duck's back. In addition to observing your ego/mind's mental and emotional reactions, I recommend you explore some useful distinctions.

Why do you want to explore and do research on new distinctions? Because that can free up your ability to view your world in a new way. These new distinctions will dispel the fog from your vision and lead you to greater clarity and understanding of the event that occurs before you. The greater your clarity, the more skilled you will be in realizing your intention in the room and not reacting to events by taking things personally.

The reason you take things personally is that you consider yourself to be the sum total of the data stored in your database. If you no longer considered yourself to be your data, the only thing left is the vast space of emptiness. At first, emptiness might sound pretty lonely, but in fact it is where our true nature lies . . . the space of being . . . the place of universal consciousness, love, and compassion.

Eckhart Tolle expressed it very simply by saying "There are two things in this world . . . space and things in space." The content of your database, which is who you consider yourself to be, is an example of things in space. The mind's purpose in life is to ensure the survival of those things it considers itself to be. The I/me/ego survives by resisting anything it views as a threat. The I/me/ego needs things to resist or complain about because it reaffirms its identity.

Without resistance, the I/me/ego would disappear, which threatens your identity.

The Wisdom of the Sands

The following wonderful Sufi story describes this transformation from the I/me/ego to the Space of Being.

> A stream, from its source in faraway mountains passing through every kind and description of countryside, at last reached the sands of the desert. Just as it had crossed every other barrier, the stream tried to cross this one too. But it found that as it flowed into the sands, its waters simply disappeared. It was convinced, however, that its destiny was to cross this desert as well, and yet—there was no way. Now, a hidden voice, coming from the desert itself, whispered: The wind crosses the desert, and so can a stream. The stream objected that it was only dashing itself against the sands and being absorbed; that the wind could fly, and this was why it could cross the desert, but how can I? By hurtling in your own accustomed way, you cannot get across. You will either disappear or become a marsh; you must allow the wind to carry you over to your destination, replied the desert. But how can this happen? asked the stream. By allowing yourself to be absorbed into the wind, the desert replied. This idea was not acceptable to the stream, after all—it had never been absorbed before, it did not want to lose its individuality! And once having lost it, how was one to know

if it could ever be regained? The desert said the wind performs this function. It takes up the water and carries it over the desert and then lets it fall again. Falling as rain, the water again becomes a river. But, how can I know that this is true? protested the stream. It is so! replied the whisper, and if you do not believe it, you cannot become more than a quagmire, and even that could take many, many years. In any case, it will certainly not be the same as being a stream! But, asked the stream, can I not just stop here and remain the same stream I am today? You cannot, in any way, remain the same, whispered the desert sands. Movement is your very nature. It will never cease until your true destination has been reached. When the stream deeply considered this, echoes of the truth began to arise in its mind. Yes, this is true. He understood that this was the only real and intelligent thing to do. And the stream raised its vapors into the welcoming arms of the wind, which gently and easily bore it upward and along, letting it fall softly as soon as it reached the roof of the distant mountains. It was now able to remember its prior dilemma in the desert and now realized the goal of its long journey, its true identity and the deathless nature of its true being. And this is why, it is said, that the way by which the stream of life crosses the desert of this world is written in the sands.

This chapter covers some major distinctions I would encourage you to research. It is better to do your own research by placing the distinctions in the viewing filter of your mind and see whether your experience of living on the planet is more joyful and satisfying. Here is a piece of wisdom given to me years ago: "Something believed is a lie but the same thing experienced is the truth."

If, by using the distinctions, your experience is more joyful and satisfying, then the distinctions work. They are no longer just beliefs; they are now your personal experience. If your life is not more joyful and satisfying, discard that particular distinction. Eventually, you will end up with some basic distinctions, which you can use to interpret the events that occur in your life. The goal is to have a set of distinctions that allow you to experience joy and satisfaction in each moment of now. You will be able to maintain your balance and centeredness, regardless of what is being said or done to you. This includes any form of resistance from any upset customer or participant in the room.

One of the essential ways to manage resistance can be summed up with this expression: "Stop killing the alligators and just drain the swamp!" Here, the alligators represent all the forms of resistance. The swamp represents spaciousness and, rather than drain spaciousness, you want to increase spaciousness in the room. By increasing spaciousness, you will notice there are fewer alligators and if alligators do appear, they are smaller and more easily managed. Many of the distinctions below require space consciousness to manage the resistance. Creating space and giving someone space is the fundamental tool to manage resistance.

Here are more than 50 different distinctions to support you in managing resistance. They have assisted me on my journey and I hope they will assist you on yours.

1. Communication and physics share the concept that *re-creation causes disappearance*. Two things cannot occupy the same space at the same time. When senders speak, they are

encapsulating their thoughts with word symbols and sending those word symbols across the space to the receivers. Those word symbols could be regarded as "things." Therefore, if you can re-create those "things" with your communication, it will diminish their intensity and energy.

As the intensity is reduced, the space moves from emotional, subjective, and illogical to a more calm, objective, and logical space. In that new space of calmness, a higher quality of resourcefulness is present to resolve the resistance.

2. In psychology, the basic technique for understanding is called *active listening*, which means repeating what was said to the person who said it so that he or she has the experience of being heard. In Stephen Covey's *The Seven Habits of Highly Effective People*, active listening is referred to as Habit #5: Seek First to Understand Rather Than to Be Understood. You can diminish resistance from other people by going into their world first via listening skills. If you do this, the people talking to you will have the experience of being heard and will give you information you can use to resolve the issue.

Opposite of a point of view is spaciousness and openness. Openness is not siding with any point of view. You are not siding with the bad and you are not siding with the good. Good and bad are relative. You become big, magnanimous and have compassion.

—SOGYAL RINPOCHE

3. *Don't take it personally* is one of the most powerful distinctions to resolve conflict and reduce resistance. Nothing

anyone says hooks or plugs you in because it has nothing to do with you personally. In *Actualizations*, Stewart Emery writes: "Our preoccupation with ourselves, our preoccupation that views everything in terms of what it means to and about us—drives us to take everything personally, when in reality other people's reactions to us have nothing personally to do with us and everything to do with where they themselves are coming from. The way they relate to us is the way they would relate to anyone who represented to them whatever they have decided we represent to them. Never take another person's reaction (good or bad) personally because it comes out of his or her conditioned reality. It has nothing to do with us."

4. *Surrender your point of view.* Surrendering your point of view in order to listen and establish rapport with another person's reality is one of the most powerful techniques to manage resistance. The challenge is that the mind is concerned about survival and the survival of whatever it considers itself to be. Momentarily setting aside who you consider yourself to be in order to listen to another person's communication requires an act of surrender, which is contrary to the design function of the mind. And yet, if you are not able to do this, you can't accurately hear the other person because the other person's communication is being interpreted through your database of thoughts.

In *Actualizations,* Stewart Emery described it very simply: "Communication (i.e., managing resistance) starts with the ability to listen, to listen without judgment. This is the art of disengagement and surrender."

MANAGING RESISTANCE THROUGH MOMENTARILY SURRENDERING YOUR POINT OF VIEW

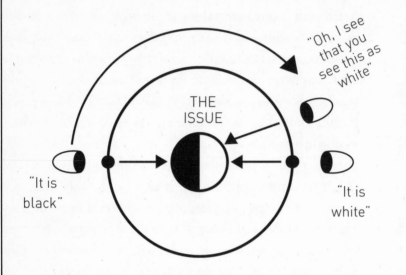

In resistance each person thinks their point of view is right and the other person's point of view is wrong. By re-creating the other person's point of view they will have the experience of being heard. One of the greatest gifts you can give another person is to re-create their communication.

5. *Listening for possibility* rather than listening to assess, judge, and evaluate is probably one of the most important distinctions you can use to manage resistance. In my experience, it seems like almost everyone listens to judge every event that occurs in his or her field of now. Whatever is said is automatically compared to the listener's database of thoughts to see if it is right or wrong. The labeling of right or wrong is judging. The joke here is that you are comparing what is said to your database of thoughts, but in the totality of all knowledge in the universe, what you know is nothing. And yet, you live your life and interact with other human beings as if you know something. If you want to have a breakthrough into the vast space of universal knowledge, then you will have to shift to "possibility listening." When you listen for possibility, you will hear possibility. You want to get to the point in your listening skills that you don't contaminate your listening by filtering it through your database of knowledge because your database of knowledge is limited by what you know.

   For example, if you were listening for possibility centuries ago when Copernicus said that the earth revolves around the sun, you wouldn't say "That is ridiculous"; instead you would say "I never looked at it that way before. Why do you think the earth goes around the sun?" You are now listening for possibility and are willing to allow the possibility that the earth goes around the sun to exist in your reality.

   A clear characteristic of a possibility listener versus a person who listens to judge is that a possibility listener ends sentences with question marks and a person who listens to judge ends sentences with periods. In the first type, the person is coming into the conversation from not knowing;

in the second type, the person is coming into the conversation from knowing.

If you look at it logically, listening to assess condemns you to serve a life sentence in the prison of your mind. If you want to break through to new levels of awareness and lead a more satisfying life, begin to practice the art of listening for possibility.

6. *Come from not knowing in your listening.* This is another way of saying that you want to be a possibility listener. The rise and fall of corporations has a lot to do with how decision-makers listen. For example, years ago, two scientists presented a Swiss watch company with an idea for a digital watch. The decision-makers at the Swiss company said the idea was ridiculous because that was not how watches were made. The scientists went to Japan and met with decision-makers at Casio, who were willing to give their idea a try and invested in the digital concept. It proved to be a tremendous success and the Swiss market share for watches plummeted. The joke was that the two scientists worked for the Swiss watch company.

Observe how you listen to the events that occur around you and you will notice that, in almost every case, you have an opinion that is solely based on your *knowing.* One of my corporate clients has employees wear name badges that also list the corporate values, one of which is *No Technology Religion.* This is brilliant because it points to the importance of being open to new possibilities.

7. *Defer to the manager.* This technique is used during a presentation when someone wants to take the conversation in a different direction. You don't have to resist; simply turn to the manager and say, "I can address this issue but then

I will not be able to cover all the topics in the presentation. Do you want me to spend time answering his question or do you want me to see him offline?" Invariably, the manager will say, "Let's not deal with this now. Talk to him later."

8. *Defer to the group.* This is the same as deferring to the manager, except you ask the group if they want this issue addressed now or handled offline. You don't have to resist because you are allowing the group to make the decision. The likely result of this technique is that the group will say, "See him offline."

9. *Re-create using mass* in front of the person who is challenging you. Lack of mass is one of the barriers that prevents the person from understanding. Therefore, in a situation where resistance is occurring, simply walk over to the person and re-create his or her communication using words (active listening) and physical objects (i.e., mass). The use of physical objects is extremely important in the re-creation process. Almost all IT professionals use only two-dimensional tools like PowerPoint slides, whiteboards, or flip charts to embody the concept they are presenting to the audience. By using physical objects, which I call mass, you are embodying the concept using three dimensions rather than two. The third dimension adds depth to the audience's understanding of the concept. This doesn't mean you should eliminate the use of two-dimensional tools. It does mean that, in addition to your PowerPoint slides, flip charts, and whiteboards, you can add mass, which will be a major differentiator from all the other IT presenters.

Eckhart Tolle states one of the greatest gifts you can give another human being is to re-create their communication. Therefore, re-creation techniques using mass and words communicate that you are an excellent listener and that you care that the audience understands what you are intending to communicate because you are taking the time to embody the concept using mass.

10. *Build affinity through communication, rapport, and relationships.* The greater the relationship you have with the audience, the easier it will be to manage any resistance that comes up in the space. Therefore, you should always be looking for opportunities to build rapport. There are many rapport-building techniques. Here's a simple formula I learned years ago: Increase communication and it will increase rapport. Just getting the person to communicate pulls a brick out and creates an opening in his or her psychological firewall. The more bricks you pull out via communication, the greater will be the rapport and affinity.

11. *Establish common ground.* This is closely connected to building relationships and rapport. You want people to feel open and comfortable with you. The more comfortable they feel, the easier it will be to manage resistance. People will feel connected and comfortable if you share things you have in common. For example, let's say you shake hands, introduce yourself, and find out the person is from Jordan. You immediately go to your internal database and pull up your folder on Jordan. Now, you can mention Jordan-related things such as Amman, Petra, the Dead Sea, etc. The person will feel comfortable with you because you share similar experiences. It lowers the psychological defenses and increases rapport.

12. *Being responsible for your interpretation of the event.* The major cornerstone of managing resistance is to acknowledge, whether at the moment realized or not, that you are

responsible for the way you interpret the events that show up in your moments of now. In *The Seven Habits of Highly Effective People*, Stephen Covey lists this as the #1 Habit. Responsibility is not fault, praise, blame, shame, or guilt. All these include judgments of good and bad, right and wrong, better or worse. They are not responsibility because they don't acknowledge the simple fact that you are responsible for the way you interpret your reality.

Responsibility is like driving a car—either you have your hands on the steering wheel or you don't. Your chances of controlling your experience of life increase dramatically if you take responsibility and keep your hands on the steering wheel of your life.

13. *Be in a constant state of* yes *to this moment of now.* Many spiritual teachers talk about the importance of saying *yes* to this moment of now. Eckhart Tolle, in *The Power of Now*, explains it by saying the form this moment of now takes is the best it is going to be. It is not going to get any better than it is right now. Rather than resist this moment, just say *yes* to its possibilities. Life only occurs in this moment of now; therefore, when you say *yes*, you are saying *yes* to life and when you say *yes* to life, life will say *yes* to you.

14. *Establish a very clear purpose at the beginning of the conversation.* Purpose is the context of the conversation. One of the primary functions of context is to hold content. For example, a glass (the context) holds the water (the content). The introduction is the time to declare the purpose of the conversation. You want everyone in the room to know the purpose of the conversation. Once the audience is clear on purpose, it will be easier to determine what is on purpose and what is off purpose. For example, let's say the purpose

of the conversation is *yellow*. If *yellow* arises in the conversation, then it is on purpose. If *pink*, *green*, or *blue* arise, you immediately know that it is off purpose. Therefore, clarity of purpose will help manage resistance and you will be able to table or deflect it.

15. *Ask "What happened?"* There is always a story and sometimes there will be an emotional component. If a person is expressing emotion, something from the past has probably triggered that response. In order to defuse the emotion, simply reply with something such as "Did something happen in the past regarding (whatever the subject is)?" Once you have a response to that question, reply by saying, "Let me see if I understand what you're saying." (Repeat back what the person said). If the emotional response is caused by some painful experience in the past, your job is to allow the person to discharge this pain through communication. This discharging will reduce the resistance.

16. *Share yourself as openly as possible*—it will diminish the other person's defenses. If the audience's firewalls are in place to protect themselves from you, then opening yourself up by sharing stories, experiences, and feelings will make you vulnerable. Once you are perceived as vulnerable, the mind (which established the firewall in the first place) can no longer rationally justify keeping it in place because you are now perceived as harmless. This basic technique will reduce firewalls and resistance in the space of the room.

17. *Each person's point of view is 100 percent accurate*; therefore, your reality is no better than anyone else's. This is a major distinction in managing resistance because if you operate from the point of view that your reality is right and the

the**broadband**connection

• • • **98** • • •

other person's reality is wrong, you will not be very success-ful in managing resistance. It will just cause the other per-son to dig in his or her heels defensively. A circle has 360 degrees. Each degree represents a point of view. There is no *the* point of view; all there is is *a* point of view. However, in resistance, you believe that there is a correct point of view, which happens to be your point of view. There is an old story about three blind men who touched an elephant. Each person was asked, "What is an elephant?" The first blind man, who touched the ear, said, "An elephant is thin, spread out, and flexible." The second blind man, who touched the tail, said, "No, an elephant is narrow, long, and snake-like." The final blind man, who touched the leg, said, "No, you are both wrong. An elephant is thick, heavy, and is like a tree." Each person was 100 percent accurate from his point of view. Therefore, when someone in the audience says, "You and your ridiculous solution suck!" from their point of view, they are 100 percent accurate.

18. *Practice the "agreement frame."* Tony Robbins, as part of his work in Neuro-Linguistic Programming (NLP), says there are no resistant people, only inflexible communicators. There are always ways of communicating that keep people involved and open. The *agreement frame*, for example, is a tool that allows you to communicate exactly how you feel without compromising your integrity and without disagree-ing with the other person. It consists of three phrases you can use in any communication:

    "I appreciate and . . ."
    "I respect and . . ."
    "I agree and . . ."

In each case, you are accomplishing three things:

- You are not negating the other person's point of view by using *but* or *however*.
- You are creating the frame of agreement that bonds the two of you together.
- You are creating an opening through that person's resistance that allows you to look at alternative possibilities.

19. *Turn generalities into specifics.* In this form of resistance, the person arguing with you is trying to persuade through the use of a generality. A generality is a statement such as "All the other customers get 24/7 tech support." Or, "Every time I call, I never get my questions answered." The words *all*, *every time*, and *never* are indicators of generalities. By using a generality, the person is trying to influence the outcome by adding the weight of established fact to his or her position.

    In order not to be manipulated, simply repeat back to the person the generality he or she used. For example, in this case, you would say, "*All* the other customers?" "*Every* time you call?" "You have *never* received an e-mail?" The person will then pull back from the original assertion and say, "Well, not all the customers" or "Well, not every time." You respond, "Who specifically?" or "When specifically?" You have now moved from a generality to a specific, which takes the wind out of the person's sails.

20. *Communicate with urgency.* In a crisis situation, immediate action will be music to the customer's ears. Once you understand the issue, state clearly what steps you are going to take to resolve the problem. You want to give customers the impression that you will move heaven and earth to solve their problems.

21. *"Why is that important to you?"* Let's say that someone in the audience brings up a weakness in your solution in an attempt to make you look bad. He brought it up because a friend of his, who is your competitor, learned he would be attending your presentation, and said, "When he brings up this feature, ask this question and you will see him squirm." Your response should be something like this: "Let me see if I understand, George, what you are asking" (in other words, re-create the question). George says, "Yes! That's it." In response, you should say, "Okay, do you mind if I ask you something first?" George says, "No, I don't mind." "George, why is this important to you?" George will say one of two things: (1) "Well, I don't know" or (2) give you some reason why it is important. If he says, "Well, I don't know," then you are off the hook. However, if he is able to give you a reason, I hope you have done your homework and know the strengths and weaknesses of your solution and are able to respond. However, George probably doesn't have a reason other than that the competitor told him to ask the question.

22. If your solution has a weakness and you think the issue will probably come up in the presentation, one option is to address it up front before the customer brings it up. You have control over the things you can communicate; the things you cannot communicate have control over you. By choosing to address an issue, it takes away the possibility of a surprise attack from the audience. If you have prepared your thoughts, you will be able to sail smoothly through this issue.

23. *Do your homework* and have responses prepared for competitive weaknesses. If you know against whom you will be competing, understand the strengths and weaknesses of

their solutions so if they come up in the presentation you are able to respond easily to the customer's questions.

24. *Defer to corporate resources* and say you will get back to the customer. There is no way you can possibly know everything about the concepts you are presenting. Therefore, it is appropriate to tell the customer that you have some ideas and will check back with corporate to make sure you answer this very important question thoroughly. A side sales benefit of this tactic is that it tells the customer that when you do business with us, we have tremendous resources to support you now and in the future.

25. *That issue will be covered later on in the presentation.* You want to create the impression that you are the leader and in control of the presentation. When someone asks a question or challenges something that will be addressed later, you do not need to deviate from your program to respond. Simply thank the person for the question and say that this subject will be discussed later on in the presentation. Also, if you are unsure of the answer, it will give you time to prepare a response.

26. *Parking lot.* When someone asks a question, acknowledge the challenge by writing it on the whiteboard or flip chart. This captures the question in the physical world, which is a form of re-creating the person's communication, and indicates it will be covered later on. People like to see their communication re-created. It builds rapport by making them feel important.

27. *End your first response with a question mark rather than a period.* When someone attacks, it can throw you off your game. I often describe this using the analogy of a boat capsizing.

You need a few extra seconds to regroup and get the boat right side up. No matter what someone says to you, only respond with a question. This tactic has several benefits. First, it means asking for clarification, which provides information. The more knowledge you have, the better you will be able to figure out the appropriate response. Second, it creates a space in which you are able to think of a response. And third, by not ending your statement with a period, you avoid asserting your point of view is correct, which usually annoys the other person and just creates further resistance.

28. *Relax your body and take a deep breath.* Keeping your physical body relaxed throughout the entire presentation is extremely important. In *You Are the Message*, Roger Ailes cites being relaxed in front of the audience as one of the key characteristics of a successful speaker. Taking a deep breath allows you to regain your balance and think about an appropriate way to respond to the resistance.

29. *Step forward or stand your ground.* Do not back away. In front of the room, you are the leader of the conversation. You are the alpha dog. You own the room. The audience wants you to be in charge. They don't want a beta dog delivering the presentation. They prefer a high-quality show. If resistance arises, stand still or move toward the person as you re-create his or her communication. This will demonstrate that you are not afraid. If you back away, the person will sense that you are afraid and will increase the attack. Here's another alpha dog technique to communicate that you own the room: If you decide to re-create the person's resistance using mass, i.e., physical objects, then use the mass in front of the person who is attacking.

30. *Pause and take a drink of water.* This is another technique that will create space in the conversation in which you can relax and think of a way to respond appropriately to the attack.

31. *Ask someone else in the group to answer.* Remember that the purpose of the conversation is to expand the audience's understanding of the subject. Your job is to contribute and be of service to the audience. Usually, you will have the answer to the question, but sometimes you may not. In this situation, relay the question to the audience. Often, someone in the group will come up with a great response. This gives people in the audience a chance to contribute and for you to learn new information. Given that you don't want to give the impression you don't know the answer, you can say something such as, "Okay, so you want to know about the benefits of Next Generation Networks (NGN) in your organization. Great, I have some ideas, but first let's give some of the people in the audience an opportunity to respond."

32. *Encourage potential resistors to participate in the conversation.* This technique is intended to build rapport. The attack usually will not come from the person with whom you have rapport. It will come from the person with whom you don't have a relationship. Therefore, you want to increase the flow of communication from people who might be potential resistors. Every time they participate, they put a little more of themselves into the conversation. This will switch the conversation from a *mine* to an *ours* conversation. As it becomes *ours*, it reduces the chances that they will attack the conversation because if they do, they would be attacking themselves.

33. *When talking back, hold eye contact with the person resisting.* This is an alpha dog technique. Holding eye contact

indicates that you are not afraid. Breaking eye contact will make the attacker feel more dominant and confident.

34. *When you are attacked, answer the question the best that you can.* However, don't go back to the person and say something like, "Does that answer your question?" Just turn to someone else and continue the conversation. Why? Because by going back you're just giving them another opportunity to take a shot at you.

35. *You can't put your attention on something and resist it at the same time.* This obvious truth comes from Eckhart Tolle's work *The Power of Now.* When you are attacked, your ability to resolve it will come out of your skill to re-create it. In order to re-create something, you have to allow it to be. If you resist it, then you are not allowing it to be.

36. *What you resist tends to persist.* This is a major life distinction that exists as a universal truth. The opposite of resistance is surrender, and when you surrender, the thing that you resisted disappears. The very act of resisting holds the thing you are resisting in place. Imagine having two people, each with one arm outstretched. Put a tennis ball between their palms. One side of the tennis ball is painted blue and the other side is painted orange. One person pushes on the tennis ball and says it is blue and the other person pushes back and says it is orange. The tennis ball will stay in place. The blue/orange issue will persist. However, if you decide not to resist, you remove your palm and the ball/issue disappears.

37. *When you don't mind being unhappy, then unhappiness cannot last much longer.* This is another version of *what you resist tends to persist.* When you are in a situation where you experience unhappiness, you believe there is something better somewhere in the future, such as more money,

better health, larger muscles, thicker hair, longer vacation, sounder relationships, additional education, peace in the world, etc. Because these things are not present in this moment of now, you are unhappy and unsatisfied. In other words, you are resisting the form this moment is taking, which keeps that form in place. However, when you don't mind the form this moment of now takes, you are beginning to operate your life from the point of view that this moment is the best it is going to get. If it is the best it is going to get, then you begin to be happy. You no longer resist this moment. You begin to say *yes* and give space to this moment. You now have established a broadband connection to life and the abundance of life's potential becomes available to you.

38. *Eliminate the words* but *and* however *from your vocabulary.* Replace these words with *and.* This is part of the agreement frame discussed earlier. Words such as *but* and *however* accompany resistance. One person will say something like, "I understand what you are saying but . . ." The word *but* reduces rapport between people because you are saying that your point of view is better than the other person's. This just fans the flames of resistance because it causes the other person to defend his or her point of view.

39. *Understand the three characteristics of an upset.* An upset always contains these three elements: thwarted intention, unfulfilled expectation, and undelivered communication. In your presentations, you are always attempting to create an open space where resistance can be managed effectively. When you are upset, you have an intention that is being thwarted, an expectation that is not being fulfilled, and a communication that is not being delivered. Just by noticing

these three elements, the hold the upset has over you is diminished.

40. *Side conversations.* In this situation, two people are talking and creating a distraction. There are several things you can do. While talking to another person, mention the name of the person who is having a side conversation. This will attract his or her attention. Call on one of the people to see if he or she has a question. Call the person by name, restate the last opinion expressed, and ask for another opinion. Participation is the best cure. Get people involved in side conversations involved in yours. Move your body closer to them. If they have no commitment to your conversation, then ask them to leave in an appropriate manner.

41. *Talk to the participant offline.* In this private conversation, you are creating an opening for the person to communicate. The person may have issues with you or what you are talking about or may have concerns that have nothing to do with the presentation. In either case, you are building the rapport and relationship with the participant.

42. *Apologize or say you are sorry; in other words, get off it.* One technique to dismantle another person's resistance is to apologize (even if it is not true) for the *wrongness* of your position. The apology is perceived as abandoning your position; therefore, the other person has nothing to resist and begins to calm down and become less emotional. As the person begins to calm down, you can pursue a more rational course of action to resolve the conflict.

In human interaction, you could choose to believe either that people are loving beings or evil at their core. If you chose to believe that people are loving, then whatever their outward expression is must be a bound-up expression of an absolute love for you. If you can master this distinction, you will then be able to generate compassion, which is sympathetic understanding of another person's pain. When you can generate compassion, you have the ability to re-create the other person's point of view. The customer, at some level, must be in pain if it means expressing him- or herself in an emotionally dysfunctional manner. However, most presenters are unable to generate compassion because they take an attack personally. And, when you have taken an attack personally, the automatic mind-generated response is to defend your position, which is the exact opposite of compassion.

43. *Please send me an e-mail and I will get back to you.* Another tactic for managing resistance is to defer it to a later date. You want to address the customer's issue and there just isn't enough time to do it now.

44. *"Oh, hi . . . What is your name?"* Say you are doing a presentation and someone you don't know throws some resistance at you. Walk toward the person and say, "Oh, hi. Excuse me, what is your name?" After the person replies, say, "Thank you . . . John. If I understand your question . . ." Then re-create that person's communication using words and mass if possible. This tactic accomplishes two things: (1) you aren't responding to the question immediately but rather getting on a first-name basis with the person, which builds rapport, and (2) you have asserted your dominance by getting John to answer your question first.

45. *State the ground rules for participation during the introduction.* For example, in a large public seminar, ask the audience to raise their hands if they have questions. Therefore, if someone is talking without raising a hand, you can ask, "Do you

have a question?" This should get the person to stop causing a distraction. If it gets to the point where it interrupts the conversation, ask the person to leave. You are in charge of maintaining the integrity of the space. In an extreme situation, during a public seminar, I have seen a presenter call security and have the person escorted out of the room. In that situation, it was the appropriate course of action. Ground rules also include restrictions on the use of laptops and mobile phones.

46. *When you first walk into the room, introduce yourself and shake hands with as many people as possible.* You especially want to communicate with the people you do not know. The resistance normally will come from the people who don't yet know you. Learn the first names of the people in the room. You can do this by having them wear nametags, putting their names on tent cards, using their names from time to time during presentation, or gathering their business cards and create a seating chart.

47. You have noticed that an influential decision-maker is always deciding against your company's solutions and is a roadblock to your success. One option is to give that person's name to a headhunter who may hire him out of the company. Ideally, that person's replacement would be more favorable to your solutions.

48. Your role in front of the room is to be the leader of the conversation. In a small group, you can shake hands with everybody. It is all right to ask the audience to introduce themselves to the group, giving their name, position, and knowledge of the subject matter. In a larger group, you can have participants shake hands and introduce themselves to the people around them. Several things are happening

in these scenarios: (a) you are building rapport by increasing communication in the space, so the space gets lighter, (b) you are learning where the subject expertise lies in the room, and (c) you are subtly establishing your alpha dog dominance by directing them to do something. In a manner of speaking, they are performing for you.

49. *The more physical contact that takes place in the room, the more comfortable people will feel.* The more comfortable people feel, the more they will relax and lower their firewalls. Therefore, you want to be looking for every opportunity to have physical contact take place. Examples of physical contact include handshakes, kisses on the cheek, hugs, pats on the shoulder, slaps on the back, etc.

50. *In a larger venue, if you know of a participant who may cause a problem, make sure you introduce yourself beforehand, build rapport, and ask one of your team to sit next to that person.*

51. *Distinguish between a statement and a question.* Often, a person may pretend to ask a question but is, in fact, making a statement. The presenter can just simply say, "Okay (then re-create the statement). Do you have a question?" It then becomes obvious to everyone that the person is just trying to assert an opinion and the presenter doesn't need to react.

52. *The customer may say, "It's too expensive" or "It is too much" or "Your price is too high."* If there is emotion connected to this objection, a couple of factors may be in play: Either you have not done a good job of creating rapport and space in the room or you have not done a good job of distinguishing the value of your product or service in the eyes of the customer. Here are some thoughts that may be useful. The very fact that the customer is objecting shows interest in your solution. Also, this customer may have attended a sales

negotiation class and learned that if he gets angry and says the price is too high, the account manager will automatically knock off 10 percent. In this instance, the counter-negotiation tactic is to hold eye contact and say nothing. Although the customer is expecting a reaction, you don't react. There is now a space of silence. The silence will be uncomfortable and you will notice that when the customer speaks again, he or she will often will back off from the demand for a lower price. It may turn out that the price is not the highest priority. Often, the reputation of the company, the quality and design of the product, as well as the follow-up service and support, are more important.

You can respond by saying, "Compared to what?" I met a senior sales VP for a heavy-duty Swedish truck manufacturing corporation whose trucks cost more than their competitors'. He is often faced with the "Your price is too high" objection. His response focuses on cost of ownership: "Yes, the initial cost is greater than our competition's, but our trucks last five years longer. Therefore, when you spread the cost of ownership over ten years rather than five, our trucks actually cost less."

Finally, you always need to position your solution in terms of value to the customer by putting yourself into the customer's shoes and answering the question, "What's in it for me?" How does your solution differentiate you from the other vendors?

53. *Here is a Neuro-Linguistic Programming (NLP) technique you can use* when someone says "You can't possibly do that" or "You shouldn't even think about that." Respond with a statement like this: "What would happen if you did?" or "What prevents you from doing it?" These questions will cause the

person to be more flexible and perhaps modify his or her position.

54. *Aikido is a martial art that blends with rather than resists the energy of the opponent.* You do not take a fixed position. You are constantly moving and using the energy of your opponent to defeat him or her. The opposite of aikido would be boxing, where you try to knock your opponent down with physical force. The essence of managing resistance is to be like an aikido master. Surrender your position. Listen to the other person's communication. Re-create it and make it disappear.

55. *You do not want to take any action that would offend the audience.* As you become more conscious in the space, your ability to be appropriate increases and you make fewer mistakes. In your interaction with the space of the room, you don't want to do anything that would reactivate or "plug in" people in the audience because they will raise their firewalls and thus reduce rapport.

In conclusion, when you practice these techniques, you will begin to notice that the amount of resistance in your presentations is reduced and you have greater ability to handle resistance when it does occur.

6

· ·

Conscious Awareness . . . the Broadband Connection

The quality and effectiveness of your communication in front of an audience is directly related to your level of conscious awareness. As you expand your conscious awareness, both you and the audience will notice a tremendous improvement in your ability to make an effective presentation.

This chapter explores four concepts of consciousness: **defining it, expanding your understanding of time, conditioning of the mind**, and **maintaining a broadband connection or presence in**

front of the audience. I'll warn you that I am a psychology kind of guy and I love hearing insights from others and then doing research on those insights in my own reality. Understanding why the mind creates time is a major insight into being able to have a broadband connection to the now. This explanation of time is psychological and if this stuff doesn't excite you when we get to the section on time, just press the fast forward key and move on.

First, consciousness can be defined very simply: the state of being awake and aware of one's surroundings. In comparing what is possible to the level of consciousness that IT professionals actually demonstrate, you could say they are in a state of quasi-sleep in front of the audience. I know this is hard to believe because it sure looks like they are present in front of the room, but this is not the case. You could say their physical bodies are present, but their conscious connection to their bodies and thus to present time is very limited. For example, one of the most effective presentation skills is the ability to stop speaking in front of the audience. And yet, it is rare to find an IT professional who has enough conscious control to create a pause in front of the audience. I often tease my students by saying, "The issue is not your speaking; the issue is that you just can't shut up."

One can describe consciousness by imagining the body as a vessel that can be filled up with water. The more water you place in the vessel, the more conscious you are of the body. The more conscious you are of your body, the more control you have. The more control you have, the more effective will be your communication that comes from your body.

IT professionals usually begin their public speaking with a very low level of conscious awareness and a very limited sense of presence in the space of a room. But why? First, because they haven't reached *consciousness* and second, because most IT professionals focus all their attention on content and are not very conscious, if at all, of the space from which the content flows. I call being focused only on content as being in Data Land and not having a present-time connection to the audience.

Data Land is the database of knowledge you bring with you to the front of the room. This includes both the data exterior to yourself, such as the PowerPoint slides, and the data interior to yourself that you learn through education and experiences.

It often appears that the IT presenters' goal is to take data from Data Land and dump it into the space of the room. The more data they can dump, the better. Recently, a VP of sales in Boston commented, "It seems like these system engineers are paid by the word." In Dubai, another VP of sales described it like this: "These technical folks like to *nuke* the audience with their data."

In my experience, IT presenters, at first, always dump large quantities of data into the space rather than focusing on the quality of the delivery. I believe the goal of presenting should be measured not by the quantity of data but rather by the effectiveness and clarity of the data transmitted.

A useful definition of communication is transmitting data from the sender (source router) to the receiver (destination router) with the intention that the receiver understands the data. Using this definition, it is easy to understand why presentations where communication is not taking place are so ineffective.

I know I've already said this, but it bears repeating: To be a successful communicator, you need to be present and connected to the audience. What do I mean by *connected*? Most IT professionals are familiar with the acronym OSI, which stands for Open Systems Interconnection, a seven-layer model describing how a packet of data gets transported from one point on the network to another point on the network. Layer 1 of the OSI model is the physical layer, for example, the agreed-upon standard of how the network device will be plugged into the wall or the cabling used. In presentations, the presenter should have a conscious physical connection to the space before transmitting the data. One physical connection would be the awareness of your feet on the floor and another could be locking eyes with a person in the audience. By consciously being aware of your feet and eyes, you are physically connected to the space.

However, when you watch IT professionals deliver their presentations, you can see that they have not achieved even a Layer 1 connection to the audience. They are focused on the data rather than on consciously maintaining a Layer 1 connection to the space. Consequently, they are not present, which leads to ineffectiveness and a waste of valuable corporate resources.

It is not financially prudent for corporations who are concerned about ROI (Return on Investment) to spend millions of dollars in developing corporate presentations and then have people who are disconnected from the physical space delivering those messages.

In order for effective communication to take place, presenters need to be physically anchored in present time. They cannot be inside their heads in Data Land. They need to have a conscious, present-time connection to the audience. I call this state of awareness the broadband connection to the audience.

The more conscious presenters are, the better the quality of their communication will be. The difficulty here is that presenters usually think they are conscious when in fact they are not. Almost all presenters are initially in various states of unconsciousness, which could be equated to having a 56k dial-up connection to the audience. The ability to download data to the audience through a 56k pipe is extremely limited compared to a broadband connection. Your throughput is curtailed, so your effectiveness is reduced. For members of the audience, once they have experienced a broadband presenter who is fully present, a 56k presenter is an embarrassment.

The question we need to address is *How do you become more conscious in front of the audience?*

This completes the first concept; now let's move to the second concept of consciousness, which is time.

Why is an understanding of time important? Because the effect of your speaking, the ability to manifest your intention and deliver your communication clearly across the space, increases when you are in present time.

Psychologically, human beings are conditioned to divide time into three parts: the past, the present, and the future. If it were possible to go through the day and label every thought that comes into your mind as either from the past, the future, or the present, what do you think you would discover? Eckhart Tolle asserts that the vast majority of your thoughts would be either from the past or from the future. Almost none of your thoughts arise out of being in present time. And yet, most people believe that when they are awake they are, by definition, in present time.

If you wonder about the accuracy of this assertion, do your own research. From time to time during the day, note your thoughts and ask yourself these questions: *Where am I? Am I thinking about the future, the past, or the present?* You will discover for the most part that you are not in present time. You are inside your head, thinking thoughts from the past or about the future.

If this is true, you are living but not being present to life.

The only time there *is* is present time, which in Zen circles is referred to as *being in the now.* The past and the future are psychological delusions fabricated by the mind.

Your goal as the presenter should be to develop your awareness so that you are able to deliver your communications consistently while maintaining a Layer 1 connection, which anchors you in present time.

This is very achievable. Right now, for example, stop reading this book and think of a sentence you want to communicate. Any sentence will do. Once you have that sentence in mind, lock your attention on a point in the space around you. Once you have locked on to that point, deliver the sentence while holding eye contact with that point. You only get to talk if you are holding eye contact with the point. At first, this may feel odd, but with practice it becomes comfortable and it is essential to maintaining a present-time connection to the space. When you give yourself a conscious command to lock onto a point before you talk, your communication comes out of a consciousness space and supports you being in present time.

As you develop your ability to be in present time, you discover that this moment of now is all there is. And, in this present moment of now, you have the opportunity to create a five-star communication experience for the audience. You will be able to wow the audience because they have seldom seen a high-quality, present-time performance. In this moment of now, there is no future and there is no past; all there is is the intention to create a communication that will have value and impact on the listening of the audience.

As you begin to explore being more in the now, you'll discover that each moment contains a wonderful sense of love, joy, happiness, and mystery. Many of your worries and anxieties will diminish. Why? Because these are future-based mind creations and don't exist in present time. Anxiety is being in your future thoughts and predicting that something terrible is going to happen. But, right now, in present time, nothing terrible is happening.

As shocking as it may sound, in order to be in present time and have a broadband connection to the now, you have to free yourself of the psychological grip the past and the future have on you.

The past and the future are psychological concepts; they don't exist in the real world. They are created by a mind whose sole purpose is survival and the survival of anything it considers itself to be. For example, people often consider themselves to be their beliefs and will argue and want to defend these beliefs. They want their beliefs to survive.

I don't want to imply that past and future are bad things because they do serve a useful purpose in managing your life situation. For example, telling a friend, "Let's meet next week for lunch" is future-based and a very practical use of time. However, the psychological distinction that I am talking about is unconsciously resisting being present in this moment of now because surrendering to this moment is perceived a threat to the survival of your mind. Therefore, it contributes to your inability to maintain a conscious, present-time connection to the audience in front of you.

For me, these benefits are clearly in evidence because I have had the privilege to work with thousands of IT professionals over the last twenty-five years, staying present in front of audiences and not getting distracted by the data. What is so wonderful is that once you have experienced being in present time, you are transformed from an unconscious data dumper into an instrument capable of clearly projecting its energy into the space of the room. You now have woken up from Data Land, able to recognize things that were always present but that you have never been able to see before.

One of my favorite movies is *The Matrix*. The first time I saw it was when I was doing a training program in Singapore. I sat through the show and I said to myself, "This movie is fantastic." I don't know why. I just knew the movie was pointing to a profound truth in life. One of the scenes that I enjoyed the most was when Morpheus offered Neo the choice of taking the red pill or the blue pill. If Neo took the red pill, he would learn the truth about what the Matrix really was; if he took the blue pill he would wake up the next day remembering nothing of his meeting with Morpheus and just go back to his normal life.

Mastering the ability to stay in present time while delivering your communication to the audience is like taking the red pill. It opens up a world you have never experienced before.

Now, let's delve deeper into our understanding of some of the issues that pull us away from present time.

One of the first things that pulls you away is that you live in a conditioned conceptual reality, which includes a psychological concept called *the past*.

Why does the mind create a past? According to Tolle, the past gives us our identity. It provides an understanding of who we consider ourselves to be. It gives us the knowledge of who we think we are. It gives us our life story. It gives us meaning. And we hold on to all these things because without them, what would we be?

Without a past, we would be nothing. No content. No database of knowledge. No database of thoughts. No database of beliefs. No religion. No nationality. No name. Just the empty space. Initially, this space may sound like a very bad place to be, but actually it could be viewed in a positive way.

For example, when you begin to detach from your need to know, you will by default move into the space of not knowing. In the space of not knowing, you are able to observe the things that occur in your life without automatically labeling and judging them.

You will no longer contaminate your understanding of the events that occur in your field of now because you are no longer filtering those events through your belief structures from the past. For example, for thousands of years, people thought the sun went around the earth. Now, if you came from not knowing, you would be open to the possibility that there may be other interpretations of the events that occur in your field of now. So, when Galileo agreed with Copernicus and said the earth goes around the sun, you wouldn't disregard this assertion just because it didn't agree with your conceptual conditioning. You would be open to the possibility that the earth goes around the sun rather than the sun going around the earth.

When you are able to put not knowing into practice, you have begun to disentangle the grip that the past has on your mind. You have shifted from content consciousness to space consciousness. You now live in present time and have a broadband connection to the moment of now. You have achieved a state of psychological freedom.

Being in the space of psychological freedom is where you want to be when presenting in front of an audience. You no longer get trapped or plugged in by what people say. You no longer take what people say to you personally. The need to resist disappears and your ability to flow and respond appropriately increases.

However, it is very difficult for the mind to let go of knowing because its purpose is survival. Therefore, renouncing one's identity, letting go of all the things you consider yourself to be and letting go of your database of knowledge, would be viewed by the mind as a threat to its survival. The mind keeps a very firm grip on the things it considers itself to be.

To let go of knowing is like allowing a part of you to die. The mind does not want to die. And yet, it is through this very process of detachment that a new part of you is born, a new space of freedom is discovered, and a new ability to be present to life is acquired.

To the extent you consider yourself to be your database of knowledge and experiences, you live trapped in a prison of your mind, alone, isolated and separate from life. For most people, this state of awareness feels normal.

Unfortunately, in our limited understanding, we have misidentified who we are. Who we are is not an accumulated database of knowledge and experience. Who we are is the space that contains that accumulated database of knowledge.

Albert Einstein points to this idea in this quotation:

> A human being is part of a whole, called by us the Universe, a part limited in time and space. He experiences himself, his thoughts and feelings, as something separated from the rest—a kind of optical delusion of his consciousness. This delusion is a kind of prison for us, restricting us to our personal desires and to affection for a few persons nearest us. Our task must be to free ourselves from this prison by widening our circles of compassion to embrace all living creatures and the whole of nature in its beauty.

Now, let's look at the mind-created concept called *the future.* The mind creates a future because it has been infected with a virus called *more.* This virus tells the mind that something in the future will make life more fulfilling than it is now. You operate your life as if salvation is not in the now but rather something you will receive in the future.

Unfortunately, this future is psychological in nature and doesn't really exist. It is just a concept you have been conditioned to believe in. The only time that actually exists is now. As long as you hold to the belief of a future, your moments of joy and satisfaction will be fleeting.

The more virus sucks the life out of your present moment. You cannot embrace and feel complete in the present moment because the more virus says you must have more.

In Aldous Huxley's novel *Island,* the people were content until a catalog order book appeared on the shore one day and they saw all the things they didn't have. They were infected with the more virus and became discontented.

You too may see all the things you don't have in this moment of now and be unhappy.

A lot of advertising plays into this more virus by showing you things you don't have and then trying to convince you that pleasure and satisfaction will be yours when you buy these things. Advertisers are the modern-day drug peddlers of unhappiness while pretending to support you in having a better life.

The media messages you are exposed to imply that your life is empty and if you want to be fulfilled, all you have to do is buy this car, believe this religion, pull the one-armed bandit, win the lottery, drink this beer, visit this place, wear this perfume, take this pill, wear these clothes, etc. Only by doing these things can satisfaction be yours.

I suspect there are billions of people who believe this.

But I also know that the possibility of joy, pleasure, and satisfaction exist and have always existed, right now. You don't need to drink a certain beer or drive a certain car to be truly happy and fulfilled in your life.

Train yourself through conscious awareness to let go of the future and surrender to this moment of now.

That's easy to say, so why is this surrender such a challenge?

Through our conditioning, we have acquired images and beliefs of the way we want our life to be. And, as we look at our life, the forms we see and the thoughts we have don't match the pictures inside our head and we feel dissatisfied. And, if we did happen to experience a moment of satisfaction, it soon melts away and the desire for more arises again.

Take some time to consider whether you resist saying *yes* to this moment of now because it doesn't have all the things you want in it. It is missing things. Why is it missing things? Because you are infected with the more virus and something has convinced you that your life will be better when you have these missing things.

Examples of missing things could include good looks, a meaningful relationship, money, education, hair, a leaner body, a vacation house, health, children, a true purpose in life, peace in the world, a healthy environment, and less traffic.

So, as people look into their personal field of now, they are unable to accept this moment of now as being absolutely perfect because this moment is missing so many things. They believe that only when they have these missing things will they be happy.

In order to be cured of the more virus, they need to give up the psychological concept called the future. Well, how does one do that?

There is nothing in the future that will make this moment of now any better, although your mind tells you the opposite.

I work on the premise that the form this moment of now takes is the best it is ever going to get. And, if I am not satisfied with this moment of now, I notice that there is something that is not the way I want it to be. Then I quickly remember these words: "It is not going to get any better than it is right now. This is the best it can be." Then I surrender and go with the flow.

I remember an incident in Raleigh, North Carolina, when I was returning my Avis rental car at the airport. As I drove up, I saw the shuttle bus waiting; I was a preferred customer, so I expected them to wait while I checked in. The clerk checking me in was a little slower than usual and I ended up running to the shuttle bus. But just as I got there, the bus pulled away. I waved so the driver would see me in the rearview mirror, but it didn't make any difference; the bus just kept going. Needless to say, I had some not too nice thoughts about Avis going through my head. Then I noticed that I was resisting this moment of now, laughed, and just let the whole thing go. Thirty seconds later, the Avis person who cleans returned cars approached me with my case of DVD movies and the Bose headphones that I wear on the airplane—and which I had left behind in the car. Those things represented about $500 worth of products. I then realized that missing the bus was a good thing even though I had resisted it at the time. Had I made it to the bus, my DVDs and headphones might have been lost to me. Experiences like this reinforce my belief in living my life by saying *yes* to whatever form this moment of now takes.

Live your life as if you chose whatever event is occurring now. You chose the flat tire, you chose the relationship, you chose the traffic, you chose the environment, you chose your looks, you chose your weight, you chose your disease, you chose the Avis bus leaving you, and you chose whatever happens in the very next moment

In this state of consciousness, you will notice that the future has less and less of an influence on you. To be fully present with the audience, the past and future have to disappear. When this happens, you are automatically absorbed into the present moment of now.

One of the important books in my life has been *The Lazy Man's Guide to Enlightenment* by Thaddeus Golas. I read it back in the '60s and his wisdom still rings true today. Here is a quote about loving exactly where you are:

LOVE YOURSELF

Whatever you are doing, love yourself for doing it. Whatever you are thinking, love yourself for thinking it. If you are not sure how it feels to be loving, love yourself for not being sure of how it feels. There is nothing on earth more important than the love that conscious beings feel toward each other, whether or not it is ever expressed. There is no point in worry or wonder about worse or better spiritual conditions, although that game is available. You will not be able to rise above your present vibration level to stay until you love the way you are now.

Once you can say *yes* to this moment of now, you will live in a state of happiness because happiness is a function of accepting what is. Another way of saying it comes from Werner Erhard, one of the greatest New Age teachers of our times, who said, "You don't get to vote on the way it is, you already did."

The mind may not like hearing this. The mind is going to argue and defend the need to have a future. The mind will say *you need to have goals. You need to want things and you need to create a better future for your children and the planet. If you don't, nothing will ever change.*

However, this is not the truth. When you stop resisting this moment of now, its form changes. The very resistance you have to the form keeps that form in place. As the saying goes, "The things you resist tend to persist."

When you no longer resist, you surrender and take a step back into a state of alert presence. You step out of a 56k dial-up connection and move into a broadband connection. Resources you didn't even know existed suddenly manifest themselves all around you.

As Tolle suggests, you no longer need to *react* to the events; you are able to *respond* to those events. You are now mentally, emotionally, and physically balanced and stable. By saying *yes* to this moment of now, you are saying *yes* to life and when you say *yes* to life, then life will say *yes* to you. If you say *no* to life, then life will say *no* to you.

I admire teachers such as Eckhart who are able to state things so simply and yet so profoundly. They increase clarity by dispelling the fog of mental delusion.

Psychologically, the idea of surrender goes against the purpose of the mind, which is survival, and the survival of anything it considers itself to be. Most people's attitude is "I'll be damned if I am going to surrender, because I am right." But if you play that game, the price you'll pay is giving up your love, health, happiness, and full self-expression. And that is a heavy cost to pay.

Krishnamurti, a sage, once asked his students, "Do you really want to know how I am able to stay in a state of bliss and happiness?" And, of course, all the students eagerly said, "Yes, please tell us." Krishnamurti replied, "I live my life from the point of view that I don't mind whatever happens." That is not the way most of us live our lives. Most of us mind what happens all the time.

Saying *yes* to whatever occurs in your field of now will give you a broadband connection to life and increase the probability of being happy and fulfilled.

In conclusion, you can increase your consciousness by observing the incredible power the concepts of past and future have over your ability to stay present. Reducing their influence allows you to increase the effectiveness and clarity of your communication.

Now, let's consider the third distinction in consciousness, how the mind gets conditioned in the first place. Why is this important? Because with understanding, you have a chance to reduce the hammerlock the mind has over you.

Once you realize that this unconscious conditioning process determines how you interpret the world, you can now react appropriately to the constant stream of events that show up in your field of now.

We live in a conditioned conceptualized reality. The conditioning starts in the first moments of life. You are born into an environment, a language, a family, a country, a religion, an educational system, a world. In that environment, you learn what things are by instruction or experience. The conditioning process occurs at an unconscious level and is so subtle you are not aware it is happening. For the most part, you agree with what you are told and then operate as if it were real. This conditioning defines your world and defines who you consider yourself to be.

Unfortunately, once you *know* who you are and what is *true*, the mind's job is to make sure those things survive, even though they may actually be false. The mind will not tolerate thoughts that are not congruent with what it believes to be true. It will consider those thoughts wrong.

You now have to serve a life sentence in a mind-created prison with no hope of parole. You are trapped by the limitations and delusions of your own mental constructs. The sad joke is that you think you are free. You are not. Every time an event occurs in your field of now, you automatically and unconsciously interpret and label that event based on your conditioning. You don't even notice that you put a defining label on an event, a label determined by the set of beliefs to which you are predisposed.

For example, years ago, people believed that the earth was flat. You could see with your own eyes that the earth was flat and if you sailed beyond the horizon, your ship would fall off the edge of the earth. When Galileo and Copernicus said the earth was round and that the sun was the center of the solar system, they were perceived as threats to the survival of the social institutions that held that the sun circled the earth. These institutions were so threatened by opposing ideas that killing unbelievers was not uncommon. Even today, we read that people are sometimes killed because thoughts in their database of knowledge are different from the thoughts in another person's database of knowledge.

You have been brainwashed from the time you were born until the present moment. The process is so effective that you don't even know you have been brainwashed. You are trapped in a prison created by your mind. You have aligned your identity with the contents of your mind, which you didn't have a choice in acquiring in the first place.

While speaking in front of an audience, it is important to realize that you are using your conditioned database of thoughts as the filter through which you interpret the world. Why is this insight important? In order to be a master communicator, you have to be a master listener. You have to be able to listen to the other person's communication without judging and comparing it with your database of knowledge.

Let's talk more about your database of knowledge. A constant stream of thought based on your education and experiences forms the database or content of your mind. In psychological parlance, you can refer to this as the *I*, the *me*, or the *ego*.

In order to escape, or more accurately, *to detach*, from the prison of your mind, let's create the possibility that who you are is not your database of thoughts. Who you are is not an *ego* and *me* or an *I*. Who you are is the space that contains those things. In your space, you have a body, but who you are is not your body. In your space, you have emotions, but who you are is not your emotions. In your space, you have thoughts, but who you are is not your thoughts.

You are the observer of those body sensations, emotions, and thoughts. What does this mean? Imagine that when a thought comes into your mind, you are lying on a green hillside on a warm summer day, watching clouds pass by overhead. You are not the cloud. You are just watching the cloud. You are not the emotions or body sensations. You are just watching them arise in consciousness and pass by. Your body sensations, thoughts, and emotions are simply events that are occurring and dissolving in your field of now.

Having the ability to distinguish between things in space and space itself can be a huge leap forward. Why? Because you would be free from the stranglehold the conditioning of your mind has on your perception and, thus, on your interpretation of reality. You would be able to break free from the prison of your mind and live with a greater sense of freedom. This level of consciousness would increase your effectiveness in everything you do, including your ability to deliver outstanding IT presentations in front of audiences.

So far, in this chapter on consciousness, I have defined consciousness, discussed time and the conditioning of the mind. The final area I want to explore is a practical tool you can actually use to create space when making a presentation and maintain a conscious, present-time, broadband connection to the audience.

Simply put, you can increase your consciousness by doing something that requires consciousness. The tool to do this should not be noticed or offend the listening audience. That tool is called *Point of Focus*.

Point of Focus is the ability to lock on a point in the room. Once you are locked on to a point, you then deliver your communication packet. You talk only when you are consciously connected to a point in the space.

Point of Focus is much like shooting a rifle. You get ready, you aim, and then you fire. You only fire after you have gotten ready and aimed. The same is true in presenting. You fire your communication packets across the space only after you have acquired a target. Acquiring the target requires that you give yourself a conscious command. This command automatically brings you to a higher state of consciousness in the space. Therefore, your communication will come from a higher state of conscious awareness.

There are thousands of points in any room and this tool works with any of them. However, the most powerful points are the eyes of the audience. Lock on and form a Virtual Private Network (VPN)-like connection with one person in the room. Whether there are ten people, fifty people, or two hundred people, you choose the eyes you want, lock on, and fire your communication packet across the space. By practicing the Point of Focus technique, you'll soon discover you are no longer talking to a group of people. You are talking to one person at a time.

Every time communication packets come out of your mouth, you must be locked on to the eyes of someone in the audience and your feet must be firmly grounded on the floor. You have then established a solid Layer 1 connection to the space before pulling the trigger on your communication packet.

It is said that eyes are the windows of the soul; because of this, people are sometimes uncomfortable with eye contact. But in public speaking, I find just the opposite to be true. I observe that people enjoy making eye contact with the presenter. The intent of the Point of Focus technique is not to threaten anyone but rather to involve the audience in the conversation. The purpose of the tool is to give the speaker an anchoring point in the space, which will keep him or her conscious and present.

You'll find a complete, in-depth discussion of the benefits of the Point of Focus tool in chapter one, "Wireless Packet Delivery." What I want to say here about Point of Focus is that it is the most effective tool I have found to bring the IT presenter out of Data Land and into the space of presence in front of the audience. It is a fantastic tool of consciousness.

Many presenters don't have control of their bodies or the flow of their thoughts into the room. Point of Focus will give them that control. It will also allow them to regulate the pace of their delivery and, most important, to create what I call *space packets* (or in IT terminology, *interframe gaps*). IT professionals are so concentrated on data that they often don't have space in their delivery. And yet, space is the heart and soul of being a master of public speaking. The ability to create space packets in your presentations will be the major distinction between you and all the other IT professionals.

When you create space, or pauses, you are able to disconnect from Data Land. You still have your data. You still deliver your data, but you are not addicted to it. If there is anything you are addicted to, it will be creating space.

You will be looking for opportunities to squeeze as much space as possible into your delivery and you will notice that your presentations become more successful. The length of the space packet or pause will vary depending on the significance of the communication packet. The greater the significance, the longer the pause because it will allow the audience to absorb and process the data.

Tips in Using the Point of Focus Tool

- Do not use a lot of words. Slim down your sentence into small parts. Give three to ten words to one person. Do not deliver two or three sentences at a time to one person.
- After you deliver your chunk of data, hold the eye contact for no longer than a second to make sure you have hit the target.
- Hold the eye contact longer after you have spoken only if you have asked a question and are waiting for a response.
- Don't talk in between the eye contacts. Only talk when you are connected to someone's eyes.

- Make sure you connect to the eyes of as many people as possible. It is a great way of holding people's attention.

This chapter addressed how to increase your consciousness to establish a broadband, present-time connection to the audience. We looked at three areas of consciousness: (1) defining consciousness, (2) how the mental concepts of past and future take you away from being fully present in the moment, (3) how the mind is conditioned over time and blocks you from being fully conscious, and (4) how the Point of Focus tool allows you to maintain a conscious connection to the audience.

7

The Art of
Questioning

Thirty years ago, one of my teachers, Werner Erhard, said, "Health is a function of participation." If this is true, you could say that the health of the conversation is a function of the circulation of energy, communication, and participation in the room. What stops the circulation of communication in the room are the personal firewalls in the space.

As the manager of the conversation, you want to create a safe space in which the participants will begin to lower their firewalls. This safe space is created by building rapport and common ground with the participants. Refer to chapter two, "Through the Firewall and Beyond," to read about dismantling firewalls and building rapport in the room.

This chapter discusses the Art of Questioning, which can be a major tool for promoting participation. The definition of *participation* is to share. Often, presenters look at their presentations as a solo sport because they are in front of the audience by themselves. I would suggest you view presentations as a team sport. As the leader of the conversation, you want to be looking for opportunities to get the audience involved. You want the audience to get out of the grandstands and into the game.

Adult learning theory stresses the importance of audience involvement in the process. People will remember up to 85 percent of what they do and say. Therefore, a major part of the presenter's success will depend on his or her ability to ask questions that get the audience to participate. And yet, the questioning skill level is low. IT presenters' questions seem to fall into three categories: (1) "John, do you have a question?" (2) "Do you have a question, John?" or (3) "Any questions?"

There are two general categories of questions: open and closed. If you want to increase communication, ask open-ended questions. If you want to close down communication, ask closed questions. Most IT professionals ask closed questions to the audience and then wonder why people are not participating. But a presenter who only puts closed bait on the hook won't catch much participation.

A closed question is a question that can be answered with a *yes* or a *no* or a short response. An open question is a question that can't be answered with a *yes* or *no*. In developing your open questioning skills, start your sentences with the interrogatory pronouns *what*, *why*, or *how*. Sentences starting with these pronouns usually lead to an open response. For example:

- Ask "*What* are some of the challenges you are facing with your network?" (open) rather than "Are you having any problems with your network?" (closed)

- Ask "*How* are you going to address the customer's concerns?" rather than "Are you going to address the customer's concerns?"
- Ask "*Why* are the lead times for implementing this solution so long?" rather than "Are the lead times going to be long?"

There are three other interrogatory pronouns: *who, where,* and *when.* They usually don't lead in an open direction because they are simply asking for a short response, i.e., *Who?* You. *When?* 3:00 P.M. *Where?* At the restaurant.

A closed question restricts the response. An open question expands the response. A skilled speaker listens for opportunities to promote audience participation because audience involvement means maximum retention. Why are IT professionals asking so many closed questions? Because in order to ask an open question, you need to assume that what you are asking for exists. For example, if you ask, "Do you see any benefits to upgrading your network?" you are not assuming that there are benefits. If you *were* assuming that there were benefits, you would phrase the question like this: "What are some of the benefits you would receive by upgrading your network?"

Another way to expand an open question even more is to add an *s* to the noun and change the verb to a plural—for example, "What is a benefit you see of employing Voice over IP?" You can make this more expansive by asking "What are some of the benefits you will receive by employing Voice over IP in your network?"

Let's explore the five different types of oral questions you can ask the audience in order to promote participation.

Direct Question

A direct question is asked specifically to an individual and has these essential steps:

1. Name the person you want to answer the question.
2. Pause (for two seconds).
3. Ask the question.

The reason you pause for two seconds is you can't assume that the individual you are addressing is paying attention. Calling out the person's name restores his or her attention. Once that person's attention is refocused on you, it will be easier for him or her to answer the question.

Direct questions are both the most common questions and among the worst questions to ask. Why? Because when the presenter calls on the participant, he or she is sitting behind a firewall, then is suddenly pulled out of this private domain and put on display in the public domain.

If the person does not know the answer, he or she may be embarrassed, which will lower rapport with the speaker. Therefore, if you are going to employ a direct question, you should have a high degree of confidence that the person will be able to answer the question. You never want to humiliate or embarrass someone in the room publicly unless it is a tactic to manage resistance.

In training sessions, I explain this by using a baseball analogy. When you pitch the ball to the batter (participant), you do not want him or her to strike out. You want a home run. In your presentation, when you ask a participant a question, you do not want a swing and a miss. You want the person to answer, which is equivalent to knocking it out of the ballpark. When people hit a home run they feel great, which reinforces their participation. If they miss and feel embarrassed, then they will pull back and not participate.

How do you know that they have enough knowledge in their database to answer the question? You could have learned about their level of knowledge during the connecting and gathering phase or during the introduction phase of the presentation.

Here's an example of a direct question: "Tom, what does VPN stand for?" The answer is not a *yes* or *no,* but it is short, which places it in the close category.

Tony Robbins teaches a clever questioning technique you can use when someone responds with: "I don't know," and you think that he or she may know but is hesitant.

Say, "I know you don't know but, if you did know, what would it be?" Surprisingly often, people will come up with the right answer.

Another time to use direct questions is with decision-makers. You want to know if they have any concerns that would stop them from moving forward with the sale.

If you see that someone looks confused, don't embarrass him or her by saying, "I can see you are confused." It is better to say, "Perhaps I didn't explain this clearly enough; let me try again." Now you are accepting responsibility for the lack of clarity and the person doesn't feel stupid.

Time Bomb Question

A time bomb question is first posed to the entire group, and then you pick a member of the audience to answer it. This kind of question follows these essential steps:

1. Ask the question to the entire group.
2. Pause for up to five seconds.
3. Name the person you've selected to answer.

Example: "Why is it valuable to ask questions in a presentation? (pause) Mary?"

The ideal place to be standing when asking a time bomb question is in the power point of the room. Every room has a central focus point, which commands the maximum attention of the group. For example, in a U-shaped setup, the power point would be in the front center.

When you ask the time bomb question, make sure you scan the entire room and make eye contact with as many people as possible. That way they know you might call on them, so they will be sure to pay attention to the question. If you don't look at them, they will not feel much psychological pressure to pay attention.

After you ask the question, be willing to wait five seconds before naming a person's name. Although this seems a long period of time, you are giving the audience a chance to retrieve an answer from their database.

The next decision is *who* to call on. You want to call on a person in whom you have a high level of confidence in their ability to answer the question. How do you know?

- Who has a high level of expertise?
- Who has been participating in the conversation?
- Who is looking at you?
- Who is avoiding eye contact with you?
- Who is clearing his or her throat and preparing to talk?

After choosing the person, you may want to repeat the question to make sure he or she understands it. Also, you may want to temper the question by saying something like "George, do you have an idea?" or "George, take a shot at it." You don't want to say, "George, what is the answer?" Why? "Take a shot" and "Do you have an idea?" are forgiving and don't require the exact answer. You want the person who is answering not to fail. By saying, "George, what is the answer?" it implies there is only one answer and if you don't get it right, then you are wrong. Having people feel wrong in the presentation is not a good rapport-building strategy.

Overhead Question

This third type of question is also asked of the entire group. It hangs over the heads of the group and anyone can answer. You don't call on anybody until someone volunteers. Once again, you need to be willing to wait up to five seconds for a response. Given that the vast majority of presenters do not control time, they will often call on someone before anyone raises a hand, which then turns it into a time bomb question. One indicator of your confidence as a speaker is your ability to control time. Waiting a full five seconds indicates you are the leader and you are not intimated by the space.

Here are the essential steps of an overhead question:

1. First, get people's attention and then give them the topic— for example: "I'd like to ask everyone a question regarding Voice over IP." Just as in the time bomb question, you want to include everybody in the room with your visual scan. Also, by introducing the topic, it allows them a moment to access that folder in their database.
2. Next, ask the question and wait for a hand to go up—for example: "What is one benefit of Voice over IP versus PBX switching technology?" Once a hand is raised, call on that person.

Of all the questioning techniques I recommend, the overhead question is the one you want to master first. It does not put anyone on the spot and allows anyone to answer. You no longer have to choose people you think might know the answer because they volunteer themselves.

With both the time bomb and overhead questions, begin with a statement like: "Let me toss this out to the group" or "Let me ask the audience a question." This preamble increases the probability of participation.

What if no one raises a hand? Here are several suggestions:

- Change it into a time bomb and call on someone. When you call on someone, lower the gradient of the question. Maybe the reason no one raised a hand was because the gradient was too steep. Consider this example: "What are the major benefits of Voice over IP versus PBX switching technology?" No one raises a hand. Then ask, "Mary, what do you think one benefit may be for Voice over IP versus voice through a PBX technology?" You call on Mary based on the criteria discussed in who to choose in a time bomb question.
- Lower the gradient by offering multiple choices—for example: "Do you think that Voice over IP costs more or costs less than voice over a PBX system?"
- Lower the gradient by giving them a fill-in-the-blank choice—for example: "If PBX is considered expensive, then Voice over IP must be considered _____?" This may seem a very easy answer and it should be. The purpose is to remove a brick from the audience's firewall, which builds rapport and increases their feeling of safety in the space. You are not interested in having a person unable to answer the question. Once the person has successfully answered this first question, you could ask a second question in which the gradient is steeper. Why? Because this keeps the energy flowing in the space.

- If no one raises a hand, another option is to answer the question yourself. However, this would be the last option because it defeats the whole purpose of audience interaction.

Relay Question

A person in the audience raises a hand and asks a question. The presenter doesn't answer the question but instead relays it back to the audience. This affords the speaker an opportunity to tap into the group database. Here are the essential steps of a relay question:

1. A member of the audience asks the speaker a question.
2. The speaker probes for clarity by duplicating the question.

As the manager of the conversation, you are responsible for clarity in the room. Probing for clarity is a technique to create a clear space for communication. When someone asks a question, you repeat it back to him or her. You can repeat the communication using any combination of words, voice tones, video gestures, and mass. These techniques are described in chapter one, on wireless packet delivery. This is a fundamental listening skill that you need to master if you want to be an outstanding communicator.

There are a variety of benefits of re-creating the question in this way:

- It avoids making assumptions. An assumption is a thing that is accepted as true without proof. As a presenter, there is no benefit to making assumptions about what another person is intending to communicate.
- Re-creating another person's communication demonstrates to the entire audience that you are a great listener.

- Re-creating the other person's communication gives that person the feeling of being known. Re-creation will differentiate you from the vast majority of other IT presenters, who are so focused on the data that they have little connection to the audience.

Here's an example of re-creating and probing for clarity: A person in the audience asks, "Why is security necessary in my network?"

The speaker responds, "Let me see if I understand what you are asking. You currently have a network in your company and you want to know why it is necessary to secure it? Is that correct?"

The questioner responds, "Yes, that is exactly my question."

The speaker now has a sure understanding of the question. Next, based on the three types of questions already discussed, the speaker has three options on how to relay this question. He can relay it using a direct question, a time bomb question, or an overhead question:

- Example of a relay direct question (Name/pause/question): "Abdul, what is one reason to secure a network?"
- Example of a relay time bomb question (Question/pause/name): "What do you think one reason would be for securing a network? Abdul?"
- Example of a relay overhead question (Ask the question to the group and wait until someone raises a hand): "Let me ask Raina's question to the whole group. What do you think one benefit would be of having a secure network?"

One common questioning mistake often made in presentations is when someone in the front row asks a question and the presenter does not broadcast the question to the entire group. Therefore, people in the back row may not have heard the question and so have no context for understanding the presenter's answer. If there is any doubt, always announce the question to the entire group before answering.

Relay questions are seldom seen in IT presentations. If you ask an IT professional what do they do when someone in the audience asks them a question, they say, "I answer the question." Answering questions from the audience is not a bad thing, especially in the beginning of the presentation when you want to establish your credibility. However, it is a problem if the IT professional never relays a question. Answering every single question means no one else gets to participate. To promote participation, look for opportunities to involve members of the audience, such as by relaying questions to another person.

It's especially important to relay questions to people who have superior knowledge of the subject. By giving them an opportunity to contribute, they will feel part of the conversation, which builds rapport with the speaker. And, as I mentioned in chapter five, "Managing Resistance," if they feel part of the conversation, they are less likely to attack the conversation because to attack the conversation would be to attack themselves.

Some presenters may be uncomfortable if there are people in the room who have more knowledge of the subject than they do. Why? They fear making a mistake and being publicly embarrassed. So, when asked a question that they can answer, they make the mistake of not relaying it to knowledgeable audience members and answering it themselves. I recommend letting these knowledgeable people contribute. If they are excluded from the conversation, later on in the presentation they may raise a hand and say something like: "Excuse me, I don't mean to interrupt, but the slide you are showing us is inaccurate and had you read the white paper I wrote for the international Internet symposium in Zurich, Switzerland, last year, you would know this is misleading information." This negative reaction probably could have been avoided if the presenter had included the expert on the subject matter in the conversation.

If the purpose of the conversation is to expand people's understanding of the subject matter, having knowledgeable people in the room is an asset, not a liability. As the manager of the conversation, you want to take advantage of all the knowledge in the room.

Think of presenting as a team sport rather than as an individual one. Get the people involved. If you do an effective job of audience involvement, you will know more about the subject matter at the end of the presentation than you did at the beginning because you have let people contribute thoughts from their database of knowledge that may be brand new to you.

Reverse Question

The final type of question is useful when a member of the audience asks the speaker a question and the speaker answers back with a question. This allows the audience member to find the answer him- or herself. The speaker's goal should be to avoid telling the audience information that could have easily been pulled from the database in the room.

Ask, don't tell is a proven teaching technique. Asking questions that guide a person to discover the answer is called the Socratic Method. When students came to Socrates and asked a question, he would ask them a series of questions that would cause them to discover the answer within themselves.

There are two criteria for determining if a reverse question is appropriate: Does the person want to be coached? Does the speaker know the answer? The speaker is going to work individually with the person who asked the question and guide him or her to the answer.

If the person is not interested in being coached, reversing the question would be inappropriate. Coaching like this is often more appropriate in a training/educational conversation where participants are eager to learn. In this situation, getting individual coaching from the leader is greeted as a wonderful opportunity to get direct input from the subject matter expert.

The speaker needs to know the answer in order to guide the questioner to discover the answer. If you don't know the answer, you should go ahead and relay the question to the audience using the direct, time bomb, or overhead techniques.

There's also another important criterion for the use of a reverse question: Is there enough time left in the presentation? A reverse question can take several minutes, so you need to manage your time in order to accomplish all your objectives.

Another factor in deciding to use a reverse question or address any question during the presentation is whether the question being asked is "on purpose" or "off purpose." An on-purpose question is directly related to the purpose of the conversation. For example, if the purpose of the conversation is to discuss network security, questions within the context of security would be on purpose and questions on storage, voice, or video would be off purpose. This ability to distinguish on-purpose from off-purpose questions quickly is important because you do not want to lose the attention of the participants by taking time to answer a question that may be a distraction from the declared purpose of the conversation.

However, there are situations where it may be totally appropriate to answer an off-purpose question. For example, if the final decision-maker asks a question that is not directly related to the purpose, it might be very prudent to be flexible and answer the question. You don't want to do anything that may offend the decision-maker.

For those readers involved in sales, remember that the presentation is just one move in the chess game to close the current business opportunity as well as future business opportunities in years to come. The sale's purpose is to close business. For example, let's say that during the presentation, the customer indicates he or she is ready to sign the purchase order. Even though you are only halfway through the presentation, stop and sign the PO. Or imagine the decision-maker starts talking about his or her son who plays football. This has nothing to do with the network security presentation but everything to do with building a long-term relationship with the customer. Listen and respond in kind. Flexibility is key to interacting with the audience. Yes, you want to follow your agenda but not to the point of excluding other people from the conversation.

Here are the steps involved in a reverse question:

1. Someone in the audience asks a question.
2. Probe for clarity. Re-create the question and get the participant to the yes space.

In probing for clarity, you are gathering information that will allow you to make a decision about the direction of the conversation. In this instance, you decide to reverse the question. After probing for clarity and being clear on the question, you say something like: "Okay, I now understand your question. Thank you. Do you mind if I ask you some questions first?"

The response to this question is almost always "Sure, I don't mind."

Your phrasing of this question is critical because the person has now given you permission to enter into his or her world. There was no pushback with the person saying something like: "No, I asked you the question." Using the word *first* implies the word *second*, which makes the person assume you will answer the question after you have asked your own question first. However, it almost never comes back to you because you are able to guide the person to the answer. You have become Socrates by guiding the person to the answer through your coaching questions.

Consider this useful analogy: You are a lawyer in a court of law and you are cross-examining the witness on the stand. Your questions are often closed, requiring very short answers. You are not leading the witness by putting words into his or her mouth. You want the witness to discover the answer on his or her own. The following dialog illustrates the reverse questioning technique.

PARTICIPANT: Why should I invest in a solution that secures my network?

PRESENTER: Let me see if I understand your question. You want to know what your benefits will be if you invest in a solution that will secure your network? Is that correct?

PARTICIPANT: Yes, that's exactly what I want to know.

PRESENTER: Okay. Do you mind if I ask you some questions first?

PARTICIPANT: Sure, I don't mind.

PRESENTER: What type of business are you in?

PARTICIPANT: I am involved in the pharmaceutical business.

PRESENTER: Good. Do you have a network now?

PARTICIPANT: Yes.

PRESENTER: What are the major components?

PARTICIPANT: I have a central office here in New York with five satellite offices in Chicago, San Francisco, Dubai, London, and Hong Kong. Here in New York, we have our core router, servers, and data center and network storage. In each of the remote locations, we have local area networks consisting of about twenty routers linked to New York via fiber.

As the participant is describing the network, the presenter walks over to the tabletop and begins to use mass to re-create the participant's communication. The presenter uses physical objects on the tabletop to represent New York, core router, servers, data center, network storage, remote locations with their routers, and the fiber connection back to New York.

One of the barriers that prevent people from understanding is lack of mass. Through the use of mass, the participant realizes that you understand his or her communication.

PRESENTER: So, this accurately describes how your network is set up? Correct?

PARTICIPANT: Yes.

PRESENTER: So, do you have valuable data stored in your network that you would not want your competitors to know about?

PARTICIPANT: Yes.

PRESENTER: What type of data?

PARTICIPANT: Well, we have financial results, drug development research, and personnel records.

PRESENTER: What are you currently doing to protect those valuable assets?

PARTICIPANT: You need a password to get on the system.

PRESENTER: Okay, so the level of security you are currently using is password protection. Correct?

PARTICIPANT: Yes.

PRESENTER: Are you aware that sophisticated hackers can get by passwords in less than five minutes?

PARTICIPANT: No, I didn't know that.

PRESENTER: Are you aware that 80 percent of network attacks come from within the organization and not from outside the organization?

PARTICIPANT: I didn't know that either. I thought the attacks always came from outside the network. I can now see why increasing the security level on my network is very important. Thank you for your help.

PRESENTER: You're welcome.

That example illustrates a complex form of a reverse question. Reverse questions can also be simple, like this one:

PARTICIPANT: Why should I secure my network?

PRESENTER: Let me see if I understand. You currently have a network and you want to know the benefits of securing it from attacks? Correct?

PARTICIPANT: Yes.

PRESENTER: Okay, why are network managers so concerned about securing their networks?

PARTICIPANT: Because the data within their organization is a valuable asset.

PRESENTER: Sounds like a very good answer to me. Good work. Does that help?

PARTICIPANT: Yes, thank you.

Rhetorical Question

A rhetorical question doesn't promote participation. It is a figure of speech asked merely for effect. No answer is expected. Rhetorical questions can be used to stimulate thought, make a point, relax the audience, or create humor.

Here are a few examples of rhetorical questions: "Marriage is a wonderful institution, but who wants to live in an institution?" "Is the Pope Catholic?" "Does rain come down?" "Does the sun set in the west?" "Can anyone look at the record of this Administration and say, 'Well done'?" An old Dial soap commercial also used rhetorical questions: "Aren't you glad you use Dial? Don't you wish everybody did?"

This completes the five types of interactive questions plus a short description of rhetorical questions. I want to conclude by discussing how to promote participation and be more skillful at playing the participation game.

In my experience, the most critical factor in promoting participation is to create a safe space in the room by dismantling the firewalls and building rapport in the room. The safer the space, the more people will participate.

People are loath to be seen making mistakes. If they are willing to risk participating, you must always reinforce their participation. You want to be sure they are willing to participate and, secondly, that their answer will be correct. Never say things like this to participants: "That is wrong." "Poor answer." "Not even close." This publicly embarrasses them and doesn't enhance the creation of a safe space.

If the answer you receive is not correct or not the one you are looking for, use an alternative approach. Consider the old saying: A student who fails to learn is a teacher who fails to teach. Maybe you bear some responsibility for the *wrong* answer. Your job is to make lemonade out of the lemons.

Probe for clarity to make sure you are clear on the participant's response. Reverse the answer back to the participant using mass. Maybe he or she will find another acceptable answer. Or you could say, "That is a possibility. Who else has an idea?" This takes the focus off that person and shifts the spotlight onto someone else.

When you connect to the next person, rephrase the question and lower the gradient. Maybe the question you asked was too difficult.

Often, presenters who are in Data Land ask questions that do not have sufficient thought behind them.

Always be positive; keep the interaction light and playful. Give hints; play a game that leads the group in the direction you want to go. For example, "The answer I am looking for starts with the letter *a*." I have never had an audience complain when I created a light, playful environment.

Rephrase the question by using the fill-in-the-blank technique: "You could look at the benefits of Voice over IP as increasing customer satisfaction while at the same time reducing _____." (costs) Or rephrase a question by using a multiple-choice answer, like this: "There are two sources of attacks on the network—external and internal. Which do you think is more likely?" (internal)

The Participation Game

Getting people to participate in the conversation is an art form and involves many factors. For example, what is the attachment of the audience to the conversation? Are they for or against the conversation? Has the purpose of the conversation been clearly explained? What have you done to massage the space by increasing rapport, relationships, and common ground with the audience? Are you trained in the five different types of questions?

The following is an example of the Art of Participation using many of these questioning techniques:

"How many of you have heard of a router?" (overhead)

Many hands go up.

"Good, George, thanks for raising your hand. What is one thing you have heard about a router?"

"A router is an intelligent network device."

"Excellent! What do we mean by an intelligence network device . . . Mary?" (time bomb)

"Intelligence could be defined as a Level 3 device in the OSI model."

"Very good. What does OSI stand for?" (overhead)

Richard raises his hand.

"Yes, Richard?"

"Open Systems Interconnection."

"Excellent. How many layers are there in the OSI model?" (overhead)

Harry raises his hand.

"Yes, Harry?"

"There are six layers in the OSI model."

"Harry says there are six layers. That is very close. There are actually _____?" (fill in the blank)

Martin jumps in and says he believes there are seven layers in the OSI model.

"Okay. Let's see if we can name the first three layers."

"What is the first layer?" (overhead)

Harry says, "The physical layer."

"Okay, what do we mean by the physical layer?" (overhead)

Susan raises her hand.

"Yes, Susan?"

"The physical layer defines all the electrical and physical specifications for devices."

"Would the layout of the pins and voltages be an example of the physical layer, George?" (time bomb)

George says, "Yes."

"Peter, what would be the second layer in the OSI model?" (direct)

Peter says, "I believe it is called the data link layer? Is that right?"

"Okay, Peter believes the second layer is called the data link layer. What does the group think?" (overhead)

Mary raises her hand and says she thinks that is right.

"Very good."

Peter raises his hand.

"Yes, Peter, do you have a question?"

"Does the MAC address occur at Layer 3 or Layer 2?"

"Okay, Peter wants to know where the MAC address is located? First of all, what does MAC stand for? Richard?" (time bomb)

"MAC stands for Media Access Control."

"Okay, where does the MAC address occur, Wolfgang?" (time bomb)

Wolfgang thinks that the MAC address occurs at Layer 2.

"Great, does that answer your question, Peter?"

Peter says, "Yes, thank you."

"So, going back to the data link layer. What goes on at the data link layer?" (overhead)

"Yes, Barbara?"

"The data link provides data transfer across the physical link; it is analogous to social interaction in that one needs to be able to talk to Bob to get a message to Fred or James."

"At the data link layer, would you find switches or routers?" (overhead/multiple choice)

Alan raises his hand.

"Yes, Alan?"

"You would find switches at Layer 2 and routers at Layer 3."

"Very good. Alan, what is Layer 3 of the OSI model called?"

"It is called the network layer and is responsible for end-to-end packet delivery, whereas the data link layer is responsible for node-to-node packet delivery."

"Excellent! So a router is a Layer 3 device that is responsible for the end-to-end packet delivery. Now let's move on to the next subject."

In this question-and-answer scenario, an understanding of the topic was facilitated through several different techniques.

The health of the conversation is a function of the flow of communication in the room. A presenter should always be looking for opportunities to have the audience participate. The greater the rapport, the greater the amount of communication. However, if you have undelivered communication, the rapport in the room goes down. What does undelivered communication mean? I have used the analogy of building rapport by pulling bricks out of the firewall. The more bricks you pull, the more open the space in the room becomes. However, the opposite is also true. If something happens in the room and a participant decides not to communicate, then a brick is put back into the wall. For example, in a training session I did in London, I used a tennis ball as a prop to represent a communication packet. From time to time, I would toss the ball to the participants. At the end of the training, I heard from the manager that one of the two women in the class was upset because I never tossed the ball to her; therefore, I must be sexist. Although I was not aware that I had not thrown her the ball, her communication about me was withheld from the conversation and therefore remained a brick in the wall.

Finally, here are six additional coaching tips to expand your ability to get the audience to participate:

1. Realize that you are there not only to educate the audience but also to be educated by the audience. Sometimes, people in the room might know more about the subject than you do.

2. A question has the power to control the focus of participants. If I asked you, "What are some of the things you enjoy about reading this book?" you would go to your internal database and open the folder called *enjoyable things about this book*. You would not go to the folder called *what I didn't like about this book*. Knowing this, you can better guide the audience in the direction you want the conversation to go.

3. When you call out a person's name, take a step or two toward that person. This movement suggests that you are interested.

4. When duplicating the other person's communication, end the sentence with a question mark rather than a period. This gives the person asking the question more flexibility in correcting your duplication. Why? Because you are creating a safe space in the communication exchange for the person to say either "Yes, that is exactly what I said" or "No, that is not quite what I mean." Just as a politician wants to avoid taking a position because it may offend a certain block of voters, the presenter wants to make the customer feel comfortable in correcting any misunderstanding.

5. In working with the questioner, use mass to clarify the communication. Mass adds depth to the understanding.

6. In the participation game, always be open-minded. When you hear something that doesn't match your understanding, probe for clarity rather than automatically assuming it is not accurate. This avoids shutting down the conversation but instead keeps it open and spacious. Giving the other person space is an act of love and compassion, which is a fundamental pillar of rapport.

This completes the chapter on The Art of Questioning.

8

The Manager of
the Conversation

As the manager of the conversation, you can play a variety of roles to increase your skill and effectiveness in front of the audience. They are all mentioned throughout the book and summarized here.

When you are standing up in front of the audience, you are the Manager of the Conversation. I use the word *conversation* instead of *presentation* because the word conversation is defined as a two-way flow of communication, whereas presentation is defined as a one-way flow of communication. People remember more of what they do and say than what is said to them. If you want to increase your effectiveness, you want to increase the circulation of communication in the space.

Host or Hostess

When you are the presenter, you are the host or hostess and the participants are your guests. You greet your guests when they enter the room. You make sure they are comfortable and introduce them to other people in the room. You treat your guests with respect and you do nothing to offend them.

Creating a Safe Space

The definition of *safe space* is an environment that offers protection so that no harm or damage is likely. Remember that the purpose of the mind is survival. The safer you can make the environment, the more the audience will give you access through their firewalls and the more willing they will be to participate in the conversation. You create a psychological safe space by being a master listener, not making fun of or embarrassing people in the room. You also create a physically safe space by making sure the doors are closed and the temperature is comfortable, taping down electrical cords on the floor so people won't trip, and covering up windows in the door so people cannot see into the room.

Participation

Most IT professionals view presenting as a solo sport rather than a team sport. I recommend viewing it as a team sport and always looking for every opportunity to get the audience involved in the conversation. Audience involvement will build rapport by removing bricks from the firewall, increase effectiveness because people remember more of what they say than what they hear, and finally, give the presenter insight into whether or not the audience is following the conversation.

Build Rapport and Common Ground

You always want to be building rapport and finding common ground with the participants. The greater the rapport, the more comfortable people will feel. The more comfortable they feel, the more open they will be, and the more open they are, the more they will participate in the conversation. The more they participate, the more effective your presentation will be. Here's the formula for building rapport and dismantling firewalls: increase communication and it will increase rapport. Every time a person communicates, it pulls a brick out of the firewall and the space becomes more open. Always be searching for common ground with the participants. What things do you have in common? For example, do you both like the same music, sport teams, or food? Have you been to the same countries? The more things you have in common, the more comfortable the audience will be with you. Sharing yourself and telling personal stories is an excellent way to put people at ease and promote intimacy in the space.

Gatekeeper for Clarity

One major problem with IT presentations is that the subject matter is abstract, so it's often difficult for the audience to understand all the terminology and acronyms. Therefore, the presenter needs to ensure that the concepts are clearly presented to the audience. This is analogous to being a foreign language translator. You need to translate the IT concepts so that the audience will understand them.

Rules of Engagement

In the presentation, there may be rules of engagement regarding the use of cell phones or laptops, participation, appropriate conduct, etc. As the manager of the conversation, if an issue comes up, you are the referee and you make the call.

Enrollment

The entire presentation is an enrollment event. At the end of the presentation, you are asking the audience to take the next step in the sales cycle, whether it's to sign the PO, attend another meeting, have lunch with the VP, or enroll in another seminar. As the manager of the conversation, you are in charge of enrollment.

Tour Guide (Guide: showing someone the way after having been there yourself)

Conducting a presentation is like taking the audience on a guided tour. You have a clear purpose to the tour and several stops along the way. Once you have finished one point, make a clear transition to the next point. In that way, throughout the presentation, everybody knows exactly where they are and there is no confusion.

Shepherd

Just as a shepherd wants a flock of sheep to stay together, as the manager of the conversation, you want all the participants paying attention. If the audience's attention wanders off, your effectiveness will be reduced. The two key techniques to hold attention are the use of a keep-alive and a powerful WIIIFM (What Is In It For Me) statement.

Cheerleader

You are the cheerleader of the conversation. Your job is to excite the molecules in the bodies of the audience. If the molecules inside your body are not excited, you have little hope of exciting the molecules in the bodies of the audience.

Is this an important conversation to you, or are you just doing your job? It is not very compelling for the audience to watch someone just doing his or her job. Hopefully, the conversation excites you and you can't wait for the opportunity to share that excitement with the customers.

The problem here is that you do not allow yourself to get excited in the room. You do not allow your body to get excited and you do not allow your voice to get excited. You believe this will be inappropriate so your default position is the monotone, plain vanilla, unassertive, ineffective PowerPoint presentation.

Leader/Alpha Dog

You are the leader of the conversation. You own the room. You move your body with purpose, speak clearly, and hold eye contact with the audience. You control the time and space in the room. You are able to pause and pace your rate of speaking for maximum impact. You are not intimidated by the audience and you are not afraid of silence.

Stay Present in the Space

As the manager of the conversation, you always want to maintain a broadband, present-time connection to the space. You never want to lose that connection by focusing your attention on Data Land.

Create space packets and ground your body in the room in order to maintain the present-time connection.

Keep Your Body Relaxed

During the presentation, it is essential to keep your body relaxed. The flow of energy through your body will be easy if the body is relaxed. However, if you lose awareness of your body by drifting into Data Land, your body becomes tighter and the flow of energy diminishes. Think of this energy flow like water in a garden hose. If the hose is crimped, little water will flow. If the hose is not crimped, the water flows easily.

Be a Master Listener

The manager of the conversation not only needs to be a great speaker but a master listener. You cannot be so focused on your data that you can't hear and re-create the communication of the people in the room. The major problem that stops people from being master listeners is their inability to surrender their point of view momentarily in order to embrace and understand the other person's point of view fully.

Keeping the Presentation on Purpose

The manager of the conversation is the driver and needs to make sure the presentation is heading in the right direction. During the introduction, you need to articulate the purpose of the conversation clearly to the audience. During the presentation, make sure that communication that is on purpose is reinforced and that communication that is off purpose is sidelined.

Manager of Logistics

As the manager of the conversation, you need to make sure the room has physical integrity, which includes everything from the materials being clearly printed to having them arranged neatly on the tables. It includes making sure the room is cleaned, as well as starting and ending the presentation on time. It means ensuring that all the equipment is functioning properly and that the power cords are taped to the floor so people will not trip on them. You want to minimize anything that may cause a distraction.

Appendix

Visual Aids

A good visual aid is like a good billboard you see on the highway—you get the message even at sixty miles an hour. Visual aids are an integral part of delivering an effective presentation. Good visuals add clarity, aid in telling your story, and make your points both persuasively and memorably.

Visualized information is the easiest way for the speaker to present information and the easiest way for the listener to process and retain it, because approximately 85 percent of learning occurs through sight.

Before creating and using any visual, ask yourself the question: "Will this visual cause the audience to remember the message that surrounds it?" A visual is not a crutch. It is a tool for getting people involved. Science has proven that we think faster than we listen. This means that, during any conversation, your audience's power of concentration can be wandering in fields unrelated to the program. Proper use of visuals, as an additional stimulus, helps you keep the audience's attention.

Here are a few general thoughts on visual aids:

1. *Image:* If done properly, good visuals will enhance your image in the audience's eyes.
2. *Retention:* Using good visual aids increases retention.
3. *Saving Time:* You can frequently save time because "a picture is worth a thousand words."
4. *Rule of Thumb:* Use one visual for every three to five minutes of presentation material. Be more than just a "reciting robot." Create visuals that enable you.
5. *Test Ahead of Time:* Whenever possible, test the media ahead of time in the environment where you will use it—especially if you are going to use a laptop for fancy visual effects, a sound-track, or QuickTime® movies.
6. *Avoid Too Much Text:* You should include only one main point per visual. Key words and phrases are preferable to whole sentences. Your visuals are not dumping grounds for all the information you can't include in your talk.
7. *Use Color:* Use color for highlighting, variety, emphasis, or entertainment value. Be careful of using colors that are hard to read like red and yellow. Be sure to check whether color visuals are acceptable in the corporate environment.
8. *Limit Typefaces:* For best legibility, use clean, simple typefaces. Limit the number of typefaces to two or three styles within a family.
9. *Remember:* Words are not visuals. Always ask what the visual will show—not what it will say.

Flip Charts

A flip chart is the easiest visual aid to create. It can be done in advance or as the audience responds. Flip charts are not as sophisticated or as professional as slides, but are highly effective when used correctly. The advantages of flip charts are that they are portable, can be displayed for viewing on a continuous basis, can be referred to easily and quickly, and are inexpensive to produce.

RECOMMENDATIONS FOR USING FLIP CHARTS

1. Use only if presenting in a classroom or conference room setting with a medium to high interactivity level. Group size should be thirty or less and lighting level should be high.
2. Use graph flip-chart paper because it allows you to make straight lines.
3. Use a blank sheet between prepared pages so the audience cannot read through.
4. Start each prepared set of flip charts with a title sheet.
5. Use high-quality markers that can be easily seen rather than dry erase markers. I recommend carrying your own markers so that you can ensure the quality. I use Sanford Mr. Sketch® scented watercolor markers.
6. Write legibly. Write neatly and large enough (at least one-and-a-half-inch letters) so that your message is easily conveyed.
7. Check your spelling! Nothing will destroy your credibility more than words that are spelled incorrectly.
8. Center the information on the page. In all your visuals the center is the first place the audience will focus. This is where you want your message to be.
9. Use simple pictures rather than words.

10. Draw borders around the page to focus your audience's attention.

11. Do not speak with your back to the group. Write what you have to, then turn back to the group and begin to speak again.

12. Write light pencil notes in the margins of prepared flip charts. This allows you to expand on items without having to return to your notes.

13. Promote group memory by placing the completed flip charts around the room so that they can easily be referred to throughout the conversation. Also, this passively reinforces the learning taking place in the room.

14. Fold over the lower right or left hand corner of the flip chart page if you want to find that specific page quickly in the pad of paper.

Whiteboard

Often you will have an opportunity to use a whiteboard either at the customer site or in the classroom. The following are some suggestions regarding this tool.

- Make sure the whiteboard is completely clean. Dirty whiteboards look unprofessional.
- To remove permanent marker, use commercial remover, orange juice, or Coca-Cola®.
- Use high-quality dry eraser markers that can be easily seen rather than permanent markers. I recommend carrying your own markers so that you can ensure the quality. Often the markers on-site will be of poor quality and diminish the image of your presentation.

- Write large (at least two inches) and use colors.
- Be consistent with the colors. For example, if a router is red, keep making all the routers red.
- Have an appropriate eraser. Don't use your hands or clothing.
- Let the customer get involved. Give them the marker and ask them to assist in creating the conversation on the whiteboard.

The Challenge with PowerPoint

PowerPoint is not the presentation . . . you are! You are having a conversation with the audience and in the IT world PowerPoint is one of the primary tools you use to encapsulate and attempt to clearly transmit your thoughts across the space to the audience. Unfortunately, many IT professionals are weak in their ability to effectively deliver a PowerPoint presentation. The purpose of this discussion is to give you some suggestions on how to improve your performance, and I will divide this section into three parts: data, delivery, and structure.

DATA

Data is the food you are going to feed the audience. Before doing the presentation you need to determine whether or not the audience is hungry for the food on your menu. This hunger is the enrollment/WIIIFM conversation from the chapter on Structure where you are determining the need, pain, or disease of the audience. If they don't have a need, then it would be a mistake to do the presentation. If they do have a need, then your presentation becomes the solution to their problem or the medicine that will cure their disease.

The next thing you need to decide is the amount of food you can feed them during the presentation. A common mistake presenters often make is delivering more food than the audience can digest. The amount of food you can deliver depends on the knowledge level of the audience. For example, if your audience is engineering people, then the amount and complexity of the food can be greater than if you are talking to an audience of sales people. You probably all have sat in a PowerPoint presentation and been overwhelmed by the volume of data being transmitted. I call it PowerPoint abuse or torture by PowerPoint. The result is you zone out and mentally give up trying to understand the conversation. Oversaturating the space with data reduces your effectiveness, lowers the evaluation scores your audience gives you, and builds you a reputation as a boring speaker. Now let's move to another critical data issue.

The number one barrier that blocks an audience from understanding a speaker's communication is the misunderstood words. When you analyze PowerPoint slides you often see that they are full of misunderstood words and acronyms. If the audience sees a word or acronym that they don't understand, they become confused and detached from the conversation. Therefore, in your role as the Manager of the Conversation you need to be very concerned about clarity. Look at your slides. Look at the words and acronyms. Put yourself in the shoes of the audience. Are they going to understand these words and acronyms? If so, great. However, if not, then get rid of them or know that when you show the slide you will need to clarify these words and acronyms. Now let's look at ways to increase your effectiveness in delivering a PowerPoint presentation.

Position your laptop so that the screen is facing you and you are facing the audience. This will allow you to maintain eye contact with the audience and reduce the amount of time you have your back turned toward the audience in order to read the slides. Set up your laptop using the Dual Monitor Display feature. This will allow you to see the slide the audience sees, be able to read both your data notes and delivery notes, see the slides that are coming up, and see the digital time display. The following are the steps to set up the Dual Monitor Display feature on your PC and also how to add notes.

DUAL MONITOR DISPLAY

1. Connect the projector to the external monitor port
2. Press Fn + F7
3. Select the "Presenter Mode" profile
4. Start PowerPoint
5. On the Slide Show menu, click Set Up Show
6. In the display slide show on the list, click the monitor you want the show to appear on (for instance the projector or large monitor rather than the presenter's monitor or laptop)
7. Select the Show Presenter View checkbox
8. Click OK
9. Select Advance Apply New Setting Without Restart
10. Start the slide show

HOW TO WRITE NOTES ON A SLIDE

1. If you are in the "Slide Show" click on "End Show"
2. On the top menu click on View → Notes Page
3. Add notes under the slide

4. Click on F5, which will return you to the Dual Monitor Display

When delivering PowerPoint slides it is useful to have the ability from time to time to preframe the slide before you show it to the audience. Preframing means telling the audience what they are going to see before they see it. For example: "The next slide I am going to show you focuses in on the three characteristics of a Local Area Network."

The Dual Monitor Display allows you to preframe by showing you the next slide.

The benefit of preframing is that it makes you look very professional and helps the audience understand the upcoming slide by giving them an extra second or two to access their own knowledge, in this case, of a Local Area Network.

Other useful delivery features in PowerPoint are the "W" key and the "B" key. When you press the "W" key the screen goes white and when you press the "B" key the screen goes black. This is useful when you want to interact with the audience and do not want their attention focused on the PowerPoint slide. You can return to the PowerPoint slide by simply pressing the "W" key or "B" key again.

Another delivery tool which is very useful is the wireless handheld remote that allows you to change the slides without having to walk over to the PC and press a button. The remote gives you the freedom to move anywhere in the room. Some of these remotes have laser pointers built in, as well as the ability to help you control your timing through the use of a feature that vibrates when you have a certain amount of time left in the presentation.

A final delivery tool is the creation of "space packets" or pausing. The "space packet" allows you to relax, breathe, think, and go over to your laptop to read your notes on the Dual Monitor Display. Now let's shift to the final area, structure.

STRUCTURE

Divide the PowerPoint presentation into three parts: the Introduction, the Body, and the Conclusion. Your first slide is usually the title slide. Use the title slide to introduce yourself and to state the purpose of the presentation. An example of a purpose statement would be: "The purpose of the presentation today is to expand your understanding of Voice Over IP (Internet Protocol)."

The next slide is the enrollment and trial close slide. In enrollment, you are telling the audience why they should pay attention. What is the problem or pain they face in their business that your presentation is a solution for? Once they have agreed that there is a connection between your presentation and their problem, the trial close is the next step you want them to take after the end of the presentation. An example of an enrollment and trial close statement would be:

> And why is expanding your understanding of Virtual Local Area Network (VLAN) so important? Because last week when we met you said that your network administrative costs were too high and the network downtime was too much. And we agreed that you needed something or some method to resolve those issues. I asked for the opportunity to present our solution to you, which is what today's presentation is all about. Now, if I can demonstrate to your satisfaction that our solution will work, then at the end of the presentation what I propose is that we move to

the next step, which would be to install our solution
in your network. Does that sound fair to you?

You don't necessarily need to actually create this enrollment/trial close slide but you do need to have this conversation in the Introduction section of the presentation.

The third slide in the Introduction is the agenda slide. This lists the items you will be addressing (which include your key points), Q&A (if you have one), and the Conclusion.

Now transition to your first point in the Body by highlighting the first point in the agenda slide. Then deliver your data using the PowerPoint slides. You can reduce the number of words on the slide by making them your notes in the Dual Monitor Display. When the slide appears you look at your PC, gather your thoughts from the notes, and then add that value to the conversation. Once you have finished your slides in point number one, transition to your second point by bringing back the agenda slide and highlighting point number two. Follow this procedure until you have finished all your points. If you are having a Q&A session put this at the end of the Body and before the Conclusion.

After the Q&A transition to your Conclusion. The Conclusion should be two slides. The first slide restates the purpose, listing your key points and maybe one thing you want the audience to remember about each point. The final slide (if appropriate) is your Call For Action or your Next Step slide. You introduce this slide by saying something like:

At the beginning of the presentation we agreed that if
I could show you that our solution would satisfy your
needs you would be ready to move to the next step.
Based on your feedback throughout the presentation

we have accomplished that goal and now I want to move to the next step, which is sign the purchase order.

In actual fact the Next Step could be many things, such as: meet with senior management, do a demonstration, attend a seminar, go to the Executive Briefing Center, become a Beta test site, etc. You can end the presentation with "Thank you" and let them know, if appropriate, that a copy of the slides will be available as a handout at the door.

This information on structure is also discussed in chapter three, where you can find a more detailed outline of presentation slides.

This completes the section on the Challenge of PowerPoint by addressing the issues of data, delivery, and structure.

Finally, always remember: You are the most important visual aid.

Glossary

The only reason someone gives up on studying or becomes confused or unable to learn is that he or she has skipped over a word that was not understood. The confusion or inability to grasp or learn often comes after encountering a word that the person did not define and understand. The more you know about the words you speak, the greater the power your speech will have.

Acknowledge
To admit to be true or as stated; to express thanks for.

Acknowledgment
ACK. Notification sent from one network device to another to acknowledge that some event occurred (for example, the receipt of a message).

Algorithm
A process or set of rules to be followed in calculations or other problem-solving operations, especially by a computer: *a basic algorithm for division.*

Analogy

Similarity in some respects between things otherwise unlike. *Example*: A router is analogous to a post office because they both read addresses.

Anxiety

Projecting yourself into the future and predicting a catastrophe. Point of Focus keeps you in present time and therefore reduces anxiety.

Appropriate (Adj., Suitable; fit; proper)

To be appropriate, to act appropriately, this is to follow the Tao. Appropriateness is readiness for the situation as it really is, and not as one might wish it to be. Appropriateness thus has to do with creation and is indeed always creative. It is creative even when it creates nothing—for it is sometimes appropriate to create nothing, and to refrain from creating precisely when one is in a position to create is itself creative. This is true control.

Appropriateness cannot be gauged or measured in terms of necessary and sufficient conditions, for the latter only exists in the physical universe—in the realm of doing and having—while the former exists in the realm of being.

> To do the appropriate is to do what is fitting or suitable to a situation. The situation is, however, in flux or change from moment to moment. Thus to do what is appropriate to one moment in the next moment is not necessarily appropriate to that next moment.

One cannot create with regard to what was appropriate or fitting, but only with regard to what is not, from moment to moment, fitting. To carry over "Standards of Appropriateness" from one moment to another is to fail to complete one moment and to set up a barrier to experiencing the next moment. This is to become stuck. What is appropriate is to have completed and always to be beginning anew—from and as the source of your own experience. Any "Standard of Appropriateness" is thus a recipe for a lie.

> Appropriateness, The Tao, the way,
> is revealed as unconsciousness is removed.

As one begins to experience life, one's behavior effortlessly becomes more and more appropriate just in the process of living itself. Appropriateness in a situation and control of a situation without force are thus identical, for appropriate action is not doing anything; it is neither submitting nor resisting. It is just being there.

Ashamed

Feeling shame, as from doing something bad, wrong, foolish, etc.

Synonym:

Ashamed implies embarrassment, and sometimes guilt, felt because of one's own or another's wrong or foolish behavior (ashamed of his tears); *humiliated* implies a sense of being humbled or disgraced (humiliated by my failure); *mortified* suggests humiliation so great as to seem almost fatal to one's self-esteem (she was mortified by his obscenities); *chagrined* suggests embarrassment coupled with irritation or regret over what might have been prevented (chagrined at his error).

Antonym: Proud

Attack

1. To use force against in order to harm; start a fight or quarrel with; take the offensive against; assault.

2. To begin a fight against with words; speak or write against.
3. To begin working on energetically, undertake vigorously, as a problem, task, etc.

Attack implies vigorous, aggressive action, whether in actual combat or in an undertaking (to attack a city, a problem, etc.). *Assail* means to attack by repeated blows, thrusts, etc. (assailed by reproaches); *assault* implies a sudden, violent attack or onslaught and suggests direct contact and the use of force; *beset* implies an attack or onset from all sides (beset with fears); a *storm* suggests a rushing, powerful assault that is storm-like in its action and effect; *bombard* means to attack with artillery or bombs, and in figurative use, suggests persistent, repetitious action (to bombard a speaker with questions).

Antonym: Defend, resist

Audience
1. Those assembled to hear and see a concert, play, training, etc.
2. Those who listen to a radio program or view a televised program.
3. Those who pay attention to what one writes or says; one's public.

Bandwidth
A term used to describe the rated throughput capacity of a given network medium or protocol. A water pipe is a good analogy for bandwidth. The wider the pipe, the more water can pass through the pipe. The greater the throughput, the greater will be the presenter's effectiveness.

Barrier
1. Originally, a fortress, stockade, etc. for defending an entrance or a gate.

2. A thing that prevents going ahead or approaching; obstruction, such as a fence, wall, etc.
3. Anything that holds apart and separates; as *shyness was a barrier between them.*
4. A boundary or limitation.

Baud Rate

Unit of signaling speed equal to the number of discrete signal elements transmitted per second. In presentations, most speakers have a baud rate that is too fast.

Being

A space in consciousness in which the "I" and "Ego" are reduced and the love and compassion for oneself and for the audience is increased. The analogy is shifting your awareness from just being a drop in the ocean to being the ocean. You begin to sense that your true state of "being" is that you are the space or context in which the manifested events or content in your life occur.

Belief

1. The state of believing; conviction that certain things are true; faith, especially religious faith.
2. Trust; confidence, as in *I have belief in his ability.*
3. Acceptance of or assent to something as trustworthy, real, etc., as *a claim beyond belief.*
4. Anything believed or accepted as true.
5. An opinion, expectation, judgment, as in *My belief is that he'll come.*
6. Creed or doctrine.

Synonym:

Belief, the term of broad application in this comparison, implies mental acceptance of something as true, whether based on reason, prejudice, or the authority of the source. *Faith* implies complete, blind acceptance of something, especially of something not supported by reason; *trust* implies assurance, often apparently intuitive, in the reliability of someone or something; *confidence* also suggests such assurance, especially when based on reason or the evidence of one's senses. *Credence*, unqualified, suggests mere mental acceptance of something with no indication of either great or little reliance in its truth (to place credence in a rumor).

Antonym: Doubt, incredulity

Blame

1. To accuse a person, etc. of being at fault; condemn; censure.
2. To find fault with.
3. To put responsibility on someone, as an error or fault.

Synonym:

Criticize is to analyze and judge as a critic, to judge disapprovingly; censure. *Criticize*, in this comparison, is the general term for finding fault with or disapproving of a person or thing. *Reprehend* suggests sharp or severe disapproval, generally of faults, errors, etc. rather than of persons; *blame* stresses the fixing of responsibility for an error, fault, etc.; *censure* implies the expression of severe criticism or disapproval by a person in authority or in a position to pass judgment; *condemn* and *denounce* both imply an empathic pronouncement of blame or guilt. *Condemn* suggests the rendering of a judicial decision and *denounce*, public accusation against persons or their acts.

Antonym: Praise

Block

1. To impede the passage or progress of; obstruct.
2. To create difficulties for; stand in the way of; hinder.
3. A sudden interruption in speech or thought processes resulting from deep emotional conflict, repression.

Body Check

A body check occurs when the presenter consciously observes his or her body to make sure it is relaxed, grounded, and connected to the floor. A body check can only occur during a space packet.

Bore/Boring

1. To weary by being dull, uninteresting, or monotonous.
2. The action of a person or thing that bores.

Synonym:
Dull, mentally slow, stupid. Lacking sensitivity; unfeeling. Physically slow; slow moving; sluggish, lacking spirit; not lively; depressed. Causing boredom; tedious as *a dull party. Dull* generally connotes a lack of keenness, zest, spirit, intensity, etc.

Broadband

This is a communication channel having a large bandwidth that allows for maximum data, voice, and video throughput. Most presenters have a very narrow bandwidth connection to the audience, which minimizes their throughput and effectiveness.

Clear

1. Bright; light; free from clouds or mist; easily seen.
2. Sharply defined; distinct.
3. Free from confusion or ambiguity; not obscure; easily understood.

Collision
The result of two nodes transmitting simultaneously. In presentations, this would occur when two people speak at the same time.

Commit
1. To give in charge or trust; deliver for safekeeping; consign as *we commit his fame to posterity*.
2. To pledge; bind; engage, as *committed to fight for some clearance*.

Synonym:
Commit, the basic term here, implies the delivery of a person or thing into the charge or keeping of another; *entrust* implies commitment based on trust and confidence; *confide* stresses the private nature of information entrusted to another and usually connotes intimacy of relationship; *consign* suggests formal action in transferring something to another's possession or control; *relegate* implies a consigning to a specific class, sphere, place, etc., especially one of inferiority, and usually suggests the literal or figurative removal of something undesirable.

> . . . Until one is committed there is hesitancy,
> the chance to draw back, always ineffectiveness.
> Concerning all acts of initiative (and creation),
> there is one elementary truth, the ignorance of which
> kills countless ideas and splendid plans:
> that the moment one definitely commits oneself,
> then Providence moves too.
> All sorts of things occur to help one
> that would never otherwise have occurred.
> A whole stream of events issues from the decisions,

raising in one's favor all manner of unforeseen incidents
and meetings and material assistance,
which no man could have dreamt would have come his way.
I have learned a deep respect
for one of Goethe's couplets:
Whatever you can do, or dream you can, begin it.
Boldness has genius, power, and magic in it.

—W. H. Murray

Communication

Impelling an impulse of data from the sender across a distance to
the receiver with the intention that the receiver duplicate and understand that data that emanated from the sender.

Communication Packet

A presenter encapsulates his or her thoughts into packets that contain information. The information can be comprised of data, voice,
video, and sometimes mass.

Communion

1. A sharing; possession in common; participation.
2. A communing; sharing one's thoughts and emotions with another
   or others; intimate conversation.
3. An intimate spiritual relationship.
4. A group of people professing the same religious faith and practicing the same rites.
5. A sharing in or celebrating of.

Compassion

To feel pity (from the Latin *Com* "together" plus *Pati* "to suffer").

Sorrow for the sufferings or trouble of another or others, with the urge to help; pity; deep sympathy.

Synonym: Pity

Complete
1. Lacking no component part; full; whole; entire.
2. Thorough; absolute (for example, to have complete confidence in someone).
3. Accomplished; skilled; consummate.

Synonym:
Complete implies inclusion of all that is needed for integrity, perfection, or fulfillment of something; *full* implies the inclusion of all that is needed (for example, a full dozen) or all that can be held, achieved, etc. (for example, in full bloom); *total* implies an adding together of everything without exception (for example, total number); *whole* and *entire* imply unbroken unity, stressing that not a single part, individual, instance, etc. has been omitted or diminished (for example, the whole student body, one's entire attention); *intact* is applied to that which remains whole after passing through an experience that might have impaired it (for example, the tornado left the barn intact).

Congestion
Traffic in excess of network capacity.

Content Consciousness
When your attention is focused on the data, you have content consciousness as opposed to focusing on the space between the content. When you focus on the space between the content, you have space consciousness and a greater sense of presence.

Conversation

A talking together; informal or familiar talk; verbal exchange of ideas, information, etc.

Courage

The attitude or response of facing and dealing with anything recognized as dangerous, difficult, or painful, instead of withdrawing from it; quality of being fearless or brave; valor.

Create

1. To cause to come into existence; bring into being; make; originate.
2. To cause; produce; bring about; give rise to, as *an adverse public opinion was created.*
3. To invest with a new rank, function, etc.
4. To portray (a character) effectively for the first time, said of an actor.

Data Land

Consciousness can be divided into two parts: *content consciousness* and *space consciousness.* When the presenter is focused on the data (i.e., content), then he or she is in Data Land. When the focus of his or her awareness is on the space, then the presenter is not in Data Land. The vast majority of IT professionals focus only on the content of the presentation and thus live in Data Land

Deception

1. The act or practice of deceiving.
2. The fact or condition of being deceived.
3. Something deceiving, as an illusion, or meant to deceive, as a fraud, imposture, etc.

Deception is applied to anything that deceives, whether by design or illusion; *fraud* suggests deliberate deception in dishonestly depriving a person of property rights, etc.; *subterfuge* suggests an artifice or stratagem used to deceive others in evading something or gaining some end; *trickery* implies the use of tricks or ruses in fraudulently deceiving others; *chicanery* implies the use of petty trickery and subterfuge, especially in legal actions.

Defend

1. To ward off, repel.
2. To guard from attack; keep from harm or danger; protect.
3. To support or maintain by speech or act.
4. To try to justify, as *he defended his conduct.*

Synonym:

Defend implies an active effort to repel an actual attack or invasion (to defend oneself in court); *guard* suggests a watching over to keep safe from any potential attack or harm (to guard the coastline); *protect* and *shield* imply keeping safe from harm or injury by interposing a barrier (he built a fence to protect his garden), but shield also connotes a present or imminent attack or harmful agency (to shield one's eyes against he blinding glare); *preserve* implies keeping safe from encroaching deterioration or decay (to preserve civil liberties).

Delay

The time between the initiation of a transaction by a sender and the first response received by the sender. Also, the time required to move a packet from source to destination over a given path.

Destroy

1. To tear down; demolish.
2. To break up or spoil completely; ruin.
3. To bring to total defeat; crush.
4. To put an end to; do away with.

Dignity

1. Worthiness, nobility.
2. High repute; honor.
3. The degree of worth, repute, or honor.
4. A high position, rank, or title.
5. Loftiness of appearance or manner; stateliness.

Discipline

1. Training that develops self-control, character, or orderliness and efficiency.
2. Acceptance of or submission to authority and control.
3. The result of such training; self-control; orderly conduct.
4. Treatment that corrects or punishes.

Synonym: Punish

Dissolve

1. To make or become liquid; liquefy; melt.
2. To merge with a liquid; pass or make a pass into a solution.
3. To break up; disunite; decompose; disintegrate.
4. To end by or as by breaking up; terminate.
5. To disappear or make disappear.

Synonym: Adjourn, melt

Educate

1. To bring up, rear, or train; to bring out that which is within.
2. To give knowledge or training to; especially by formal schooling, teaching, or training
3. Knowledge, ability, etc.

Synonym: To make conscious that which is unconscious. A drawing out from the person of something that is already there in an idle state, and not filling up of an empty container with knowledge.

Effect

A change that is a result or consequence of an action or other cause.

Effective

1. Producing a definite or desired result.
2. Efficient.

Synonym: Effective is applied to that which produces a definite effect or result (an effective speaker).

Embarrass

1. To cause to feel self-conscious, confused, and ill at ease; disconcert; fluster.
2. To hinder, impede; cause difficulties to.
3. To complicate; make more difficult.

Synonym:
Embarrass is to feel ill at ease so as to result in a loss of composure (embarrassed by their compliments). *Abash* implies a sudden loss of self-confidence and a growing feeling of shame and inadequacy (I stood abashed at his rebuke); *discomfit* implies a frustration of plans or expectations and often connotes a resultant feeling of

discomposure or humiliation; to *disconcert* is to cause to lose quickly one's self-possession so as to result in confusion or mental disorganization (his interruptions were disconcerting); *disorganization*; *rattle* and *faze* are colloquial equivalents for disconcert, but the former emphasizes emotional agitation, and the latter is most commonly used in negative constructions (danger does not faze him).

Antonym: Compose, assure

Encryption

Application of a specific algorithm to data so as to alter the appearance of the data, making it incomprehensible to those who are not authorized to see the information.

The role of the presenter is to strive for clarity and yet at times the presenter encrypts the data to make it incomprehensible to the audience.

Enlist

To win the support of; to get the help or service of, as *we will enlist him in our movement*; to join or support a cause or movement.

Enroll

1. To record in a list.
2. To enlist.
3. To accept as a member; make a person a member.
4. Create a compelling future that draws a person to it.
5. Identify customer pain (current, past, future), purpose to heal the pain, pleasure is to satisfy customer pain.

To enroll is to enter your own or somebody else's name on an official register.

Another definition of enrollment is standing in the future and grasping a possibility, then turning around and showing that possibility to the audience. When the audience sees that possibility, they experience value and pleasure and move toward that possibility. They believe that the possibility that is your conversation will reduce their fears, relieve their pain, and solve their business problem to help them meet their goals.

Entanglement

To involve in or as in a tangle; catch, as in a net, vine, etc., so that escape is difficult; ensnare.

1. To involve in difficulty.
2. To confuse mentally; perplex.
3. To cause to be tangled; complicate.

Entertain

1. To hold the attention of; interest; divert; amuse.
2. To give hospitality to; have as a guest.

Synonym: Amuse

Enthusiasm

To be inspired, be possessed by God, inspire.

1. Originally, supernatural inspiration or possession; inspired prophetic or poetic ecstasy.
2. Intense or eager interest; zeal; fervor.
3. Something arousing such interest or zeal.
4. Religious frenzy.

Synonym: Passion

Environment

Something that surrounds. All the conditions, circumstances, and influences surrounding and affecting the development of an organism or group of organisms.

Exaggerate

To increase or enlarge to an abnormal degree; overemphasize, intensify.

Excite

1. To put into motion or activity; stir up.
2. To arouse; call forth; provoke.

Synonym: Provoke

Expand

1. To spread out; open out; stretch out; unfold.
2. To cause to fill more space; increase in size.

Expectation

1. A looking forward to; anticipation.
2. A looking for as due, proper, or necessary.
3. A reason or warrant for looking forward to something.

Fail

1. To be lacking or insufficient; fall short.
2. To lose power or strength; weaken; die away.
3. To be deficient or negligent in an obligation, duty, or expectation; default.
4. To be unsuccessful in obtaining a desired end; be unable to do or become; miss.

Faithful

Keeping faith; worthy of trust; honest; loyal.

1. Reliable, dependable.
2. Accurate; exact; true, as a faithful copy.

Synonym:
Faithful implies continued, steadfast adherence to a person or thing to whom one is bound by an oath, duty, obligation, etc. (a faithful spouse); *loyal* implies undeviating allegiance to a person, cause, institution, etc., which one feels morally bound to support or defend (a loyal friend); *constant* suggests freedom from fickleness in affections or loyalties (a constant lover); *stanch* (or *staunch*) implies such strong allegiance to one's principles or purpose as not to be turned aside by any cause (a stanch defender of the truth); *resolute* stresses unwavering determination, often in adhering to one's personal ends or aims (she was resolute in her decision to stay).

Antonym: Faithless

Faithless

Not keeping faith; dishonest, disloyal. Unreliable, undependable.

Synonym:
Faithless implies failure to adhere to an oath, duty, obligation, etc. (a faithless spouse); *false*, in this connection more or less synonymous with faithless, stresses failure in devotion to someone or something that has a moral claim to one's support (a false friend); *disloyal* implies a breach of allegiance to a person, cause, institution, etc. (disloyal to one's family); *traitorous* strictly implies the commission

of an act of treason; *treacherous* suggests an inclination to commit treason or a tendency to betray a trust (his treacherous colleagues); *perfidious* adds to the meaning of treacherous, a connotation of sordidness or depravity (a perfidious informer).

Antonym: Faithful

Fear

1. A feeling of anxiety and agitation caused by the presence or perceived presence or nearness of danger, evil, pain, etc.
2. A feeling of uneasiness, disquiet, anxiety, concern.

Synonym:
Fear is the general term for the anxiety and agitation felt at the presence of danger; *dread* refers to the fear of depression felt in anticipating something dangerous or disagreeable (to live in dread of poverty); *fright* applies to a sudden, shocking, usually momentary fear (the mouse gave her a fright); *alarm* implies the fright felt at the sudden realization of danger (he felt alarm at the sight of the pistol); *dismay* implies a loss of courage or a feeling of consternation at the prospect of trouble or danger; *terror* implies an overwhelming, often paralyzing fear (the terror of soldiers in combat); *panic* refers to a frantic, unreasoning fear, often one that spreads quickly and leads to irrational, aimless action (the cry "FIRE" created a panic).

Firewall

1. A device or a software package that separates more secure network components from less secure components, protecting the more secure network from inappropriate access.
2. A router or access server designated as a buffer between any connected public network and a private network. A firewall router

uses access lists and other methods to ensure the security of the private network.

Focal Point

Every room has a place where the leader should stand. It should be centered and in front of the audience. During the introduction and conclusion, it looks polished and professional to be standing in this focal point of the room.

Fool

A person with little or no judgment, common sense, wisdom, etc.; simpleton.

Forgive

1. To give up resentment against or the desire to punish; stop being angry with; pardon.
2. To give up all claim to punish or exact penalty for.

Frame

Logical grouping of information sent as a data link layer unit over a transmission medium.

Freedom

The power or right to act, speak, or think as one wants without hindrance or restraint. The state of not being imprisoned or enslaved.

Grace

1. Good will; favor.
2. The love and favor of God toward man.
3. Unmerited help given to people by God.

Guest

1. A person entertained at the home or table of another; visitor.

2. A person receiving the hospitality of a club, institution, etc., of which he is not a member.

Hello Packet
A packet that is used by routers for neighbor discovery and recovery. Hello packets also indicate that a client is still operating and network ready.

Hop
Passage of a data packet between two network nodes (for example, between two routers).

Hospitable
1. Entertaining, or fond of entertaining, guests in a friendly way; generous manner.
2. Caused or characterized by generosity and friendliness to guests, as *a hospitable act.*
3. Liberal and generous in disposition and mind; receptive or open, as to new ideas.

Host (Hostess)
Someone who entertains guests in his/her home or at his/her own expense. The person who initiates or presides over any social gathering.

Inhibition
Psychological process that restrains or suppresses an action, emotion, or thought.

Inspire
1. Originally to breathe or blow upon or into; to infuse (life into) by breathing.
2. To draw (air) into the lungs; inhale, opposite of expire.

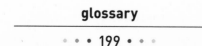

3. To have an animating effect upon; influence, stimulate, or impel, especially to stimulate or impel to some creative effort.
4. To cause, guide, communicate, or motivate by divine influence, as *God inspired the scriptures*.
5. To arouse or produce (a thought or feeling).

Integrity

1. The quality or state of being complete; unbroken condition; soundness.
2. The quality or state of being unimpaired; perfect condition.
3. The quality or state of sound moral principle; uprightness; honesty and sincerity.

Integrity implies an incorruptible soundness of moral character, especially as displayed to fulfilling trusts.

Intention

1. An intending, determination to do a specified thing or act in a specified manner.
2. Anything intended; ultimate end or purpose, as in *What is your intention?*

Synonym:
Intention is the general word implying a having something in mind as a plan or design or referring to the plan had in mind; *intent* is a somewhat formal term now largely in legal usage, connotes more deliberation (assault with intent to kill); *purpose* connotes greater resolution or determination in the plan (I have a purpose in writing you); *aim* refers to a specific intention and connotes a directing of all efforts toward this; *goal* suggests laborious effort in striving to attain something; *end* emphasizes the final result one hopes to achieve as

distinguished from the process of achieving it; *object* is used for an end that is the direct result of a need or desire; *objective* refers to a specific end that is capable of being reached.

Interface
Connection between two systems or devices.

Interframe Gap (Also known as Interpacket Gap)
Ethernet devices must allow a minimum idle period between transmission of Ethernet frames known as the interframe gap (IFG) or interpacket gap (IPG). It provides a brief recovery time between frames to allow devices to prepare for reception of the next frame.

Intrusion Detection
Security service that monitors and analyzes system events for the purpose of finding (and providing real-time or near real-time warnings of) attempts to access system resources in an unauthorized manner.

Involve
1. To make intricate, tangled, or complicated.
2. To entangle in trouble, difficulty, danger, etc.; implicate.
3. To draw or hold within itself; include (for example, a riot that soon involved thousands).
4. To relate to or affect (for example, his honor is involved).
5. To make busy, employ; occupy (for example, involved in research).

Keep-alive
Message sent by one network device to inform another network device that the virtual circuit between the two is still active.

Latency

1. The delay between the time a device requests access to a network and the time it is granted permission to transmit.
2. Delay between the time a device receives a frame and the time that frame is forwarded out of the destination port.

Listening

To listen to the *listening* of the audience means for the presenter to understand the business concerns, company politics, and even cultural background of the audience.

Logistics

The logistics of deploying forces in Afghanistan refers to the organization, planning, plans, management, arrangement, administration, orchestration, coordination, execution, handling, and running.

Loyal

1. Faithful to the constituted authority of one's county.
2. Faithful to those persons, ideals, etc. that one is under.
3. Obligation to defend or support.
4. Relating to or indicating loyalty.

Synonym: Faithful

Metaphor

A figure of speech in which one thing is likened to another, different thing by being spoken of as if it were that other; implied comparison, for example, *All the world is a stage* or *The ship plowed the sea.*

Mindfulness

Mindfulness is being present in each moment of now. It is a friendly, nonjudging, allowing, present-moment awareness. It is similar to stillness, which is awareness without thought. In a mindful state of consciousness, when an emotion or thought arises, you are able to observe it and not react to it. It is just like a mirror that reflects whatever comes before it. Mindfulness is not for or against anything. It doesn't try to add or subtract, to improve or change in any way.

Miracle
Incident, event, or action that apparently contradicts known scientific laws and is hence thought to be due to supernatural causes. An extraordinary event manifesting divine intervention in human affairs.

Node
Term used generically to refer to any entity that can access a network, and frequently is used interchangeably with *device*.

Open System Interconnection
The OSI reference model describes how information from a software application in one computer moves through a network medium to a software application in another computer. The OSI reference model is a conceptual model composed of seven layers, each specifying particular network functions.

- Layer 7—Application
- Layer 6—Presentation
- Layer 5—Session
- Layer 4—Transport
- Layer 3—Network
- Layer 2—Data link

In presentations, the data link layer equates to the reliable transit of data across the wireless network link. The Media Access Control (MAC Address), which is a sub-layer of the data link layer, would be the name of the person to whom you are talking. Flow control would be the correct rate and pace of your delivery and the data link layer would also provide for the correct sequencing of your communication packets.

- Layer 1—Physical

In presentations the physical layer would equate to having a conscious connection to your physical body (especially feeling your feet on the floor) and a conscious connection to a point in the space. Conscious awareness of your body would occur during a body check. The most powerful point in the space would be the eyes of someone in the audience. Because there is not an actual physical connection between the sender and receiver, you could say that public speaking is the integration and transmission of data, voice, and video over a wireless Local Area Network.

Paradox

A statement, proposition, or situation that seems to be absurd or contradictory, but in fact is or may be true.

Passion

1. The state or power of receiving or being affected by outside influences.
2. Any one of the emotions, as hate, grief, love, fear, joy, etc.
3. Extreme, compelling emotion; intense emotional drive or excitement.
4. The object of any strong desire or fondness.

Synonym:
Passion usually implies a strong emotion that has an overpowering or compelling effect (his passions overcame his reason); *fervor* and

ardor both imply emotion of burning intensity; fervor suggesting a constant glow of feelings (religious fervor) and ardor, a restless, flame-like emotion (the ardor of youth); *enthusiasm* implies strongly favorable feelings for an object or cause and usually suggests eagerness in the pursuit of something (his enthusiasm for golf); *zeal* implies intense enthusiasm for an object or cause, usually as displayed in vigorous and untiring activity in its support (inflamed with a zeal for reform).

Philosophy
Branch of knowledge or academic study devoted to the systematic examination of basic concepts as truth, existence, reality, causality, and freedom.

Power
1. Ability to do; capacity to act; capability of performing or producing.
2. A specific ability or faculty, as *the power of healing.*
3. Great ability to do, act, or affect strongly.
4. The ability to control others; authority; sway; influence a person or thing; having great influence, force, or authority.

Synonym:
Power denotes the inherent ability or the admitted right to rule, govern, determine, etc. (the limited power of the president); *authority* refers to the power, because of rank or office; to give commands, enforce obedience (the authority of a teacher); *jurisdiction* refers to the power to rule or decide within certain defined limits (the jurisdiction of the courts); *dominion* implies sovereign or supreme authority (dominion over a dependent state); *sway* stresses the predominance of sweeping scope of power (the Romans held sway over the ancient

world); *control* implies authority to regulate, restrain, or curb (under the control of a guardian); *command* implies such authority that enforces obedience to one's orders (in command of a regiment).

Praise

1. To commend the worth of; express approval or admiration of.
2. To laud the glory of (God), as in song; glorify; extol.

Synonym:

Praise is the simple, basic word implying an expression of approval, esteem, or commendation (to praise one's performance); *laud* implies great, sometimes extravagant praise (the critics lauded the actor to the skies); *acclaim* suggests an outward show of strong approval, as by loud applause, cheering, etc. (he was acclaimed the victor); *extol* implies exalting of lofty praise (the scientist was extolled for his work); *eulogize* suggests formal praise in speech or writing (the minister eulogized the exemplary life of the deceased).

Present

To offer to view or notice; exhibit; display; show.

Present Time

Time can be divided into three parts: the past, the present, and the future. Present time or being in the *now* happens when you fully surrender to whatever form this moment of now takes. Your attitude is that this moment of now is a self-contained frame in which you are going to establish a VPN tunnel to the other person, and create and deliver your communication. You are not going to create and deliver another communication until this moment of connection is totally complete. In the act of presenting you are totally present in the now. You are not thinking about the future or the past but rather focusing on creating your communication in the present moment. And it is during the creation of the space packet that you look at your interior database of knowledge and upload your next communication packet into the public domain.

Protocol
Formal description of a set of rules and conventions that govern how devices on a network exchange information. This would be analogous to two people agreeing to speak French so they can clearly exchange their thoughts. In this situation, the French language would be the agreed-upon protocol.

Provoke
1. To excite to some action or feeling.
2. To anger; irritate.
3. To stir up (action or feeling).
4. To call forth; evoke.

Synonym:
Provoke implies rather generally an arousing to some action or feeling (thought-provoking); *excite* suggests a more powerful or profound stirring or moving of the thoughts or emotions (it excites my imagination); *stimulate* implies an arousing as if by goading or pricking and hence, often connotes a bringing out of a state of inactivity or indifference (to stimulate one's enthusiasm); *pique* suggests a stimulating as if by irritating (to pique one's curiosity).

See: Irritate

Purpose
1. Something one intends to get or to do; intention; aim.
2. Resolution, determination.

3. The object for which something exists or is done; end in view. An idea kept before the mind as an end of being there.

Synonym: Intend; intention

Rapport
A harmonious, empathetic, or sympathetic relation or connection to another self. An accord or affinity.

Regret
A troubled feeling or remorse over something that has happened, especially over something that one has done or left undone.

Synonym:
Remorse is a deep, torturing sense of guilt felt over a wrong that one has done; self-reproach.

Rejection
1. To throw or fling back.
2. Refuse to take, agree to, accede to, use, believe, etc.
3. To discard; throw out or away as useless or substandard.
4. To rebuff.

Relationship
1. An understanding and being aware of another person's way of being.
2. The condition of understanding and being aware of another person.
3. The condition of being connected (joined or coupled) or associated (sharing mutual participation) through affinity (natural liking for).

Relax

Make or become less tense or anxious.

Relax Response

A term coined by Herbert Benson, a researcher at Harvard Medical School, in studies on transcendental meditation. In a meditative state, people would be able to slow their heart rate and breathing. The blood pressure comes down. Muscles soften and relax. There is a growing sense of ease and calm in the body and mind.

Resentment

A feeling of bitter hurt or indignation from a sense of being injured or offended.

To resent is to feel a bitter hurt or indignation at some act, remark, etc. or toward a person from a sense of being injured or offended.

Resistance

Opposition that a circuit, component, or substance presents to the flow of electricity.

Responsibility

> Responsibility starts with the willingness to acknowledge that you are cause in the matter. It starts with the willingness to deal with a situation from and with the point of view, whether at the moment realized or not, that you are the source of what you are, what you do, and what you have. This point of view extends to include even what is done to you and ultimately what another does to another. Responsibility is not fault, praise, blame, shame, or

guilt. All these include judgments and evaluations of good and bad, right and wrong, better or worse. They are not responsibility as they are all beyond a simple acknowledgment that you are cause in your own experience.

—Werner Erhard

Result
Anything that comes about as a consequence or outcome of some action, process, etc.

Router
Network layer device that determines the optimal path along which network traffic should be forwarded.

Sacrifice
Sacrifice is the act of giving up, destroying, permitting injury to, or forgoing something valued for the sake of something having a more pressing claim.

Satisfy
1. To fulfill or answer the requirements or conditions of something.
2. To fulfill the needs, wishes, or desires of someone; intent; gratify.
3. To comply with; to free from doubt or anxiety; to answer a doubt or objection adequately; solve.
4. To give what is due to.

Synonym:
Satisfy implies complete fulfillment of one's wishes, needs, expectations, etc.; *content* implies a filling of requirements to the degree that one is not disturbed by a desire for something more or different (for

example, some persons are satisfied only by great wealth; others are content with a modest but secure income).

Service

Conduct giving assistance or advantage to another or others.

> I don't know what your destiny will be,
> But one thing I know; the only ones among you
> Who will be really happy are those who have sought
> And found how to serve.
>
> —Albert Schweitzer

Share

1. A part or portion that is allotted or belongs to an individual; part contributed by one.
2. A just, due, reasonable, or full share, as, *everyone has done his share of work, we had our share of laughs.*

Synonym:

Share means to use, enjoy, possess, etc. in common with others and generally connotes a giving or receiving a part of something (to share expenses, glory, etc.); *participate* implies a taking part with others in some activity, enterprise, etc. (to participate in talks); *partake* implies a taking one's share, as of a meal, responsibility, etc. (to partake of a friend's hospitality).

Space Consciousness

A person has space consciousness when his or her awareness is not on the content (that is, things or data), but rather on the spaces between the content. In that space, there is no speaking.

Space Packet

A space packet can also be referred to as a pause, space of stillness, or an Interframe Gap. It occurs between communication packets, which carry the data. The length of the space packet depends on the importance of the point being made. The more important, the longer you pause, which then allows the audience to absorb and think about the data.

Stillness

Eckhart Tolle refers to stillness as consciousness without thought. It is the current of awareness, which is a different frequency than data. Every time an IT professional delivers data, it disturbs the stillness of the space. The stillness of the space returns when the presenter generates space packets.

Subtle

Slight and not obvious; cleverly indirect and ingenious.

Suppress

To put down by authority or force; subdue; to keep from being known; to hold back.

Surrender

1. To give up possession of or power over; yield to another on demand or compulsion; to give up or abandon, as in *We surrendered all hope.*
2. To give oneself up to another's power or control, especially as a prisoner.
3. To momentarily surrender your point of view to duplicate another's.

Synonym:

Surrender commonly implies the giving up of something completely after striving to keep it (to surrender a fort, one's freedom, etc.); *relinquish* is the general word implying an abandoning, giving up, or letting go of something held (to relinquish one's grasp, a claim, etc.); *yield* is to concede or give way under pressure (to yield one's consent); *submit* is to give in to authority or superior force (to submit to a conqueror); *resign* implies a voluntary, formal relinquishment and used reflexively, connotes submission or passive acceptance (to resign an office, to resign oneself to failure).

Survive

To live or exist longer than or beyond the life or existence of; outlive.

Synchronization

Establishment of a common timing between a sender and a receiver.

Throughput

Rate of information arriving at, and possibly passing through, a particular point in a network system.

Thwarted

Hindered, blunted or obstructed, frustrated or defeated.

Token

In a Local Area Network a node can transmit only when in possession of a sequence of bits (called the token) that is passed to each node in turn. This is a characteristic of a Token Ring Network.

Undelivered

1. Held back from giving forth or expressing in words.
2. Withheld, not emitted or discharged.
3. Not carried to and left at the proper place.

Unfulfilled

1. Not meeting the requirements of.
2. Not satisfied.
3. Not carried out as promised or desired.
4. Not realized completely, as an ambition.

Upset

1. To disturb the functioning, fulfillment, or completion of.
2. To disturb mentally or emotionally, or physically make sick.
3. To overturn or overthrow, especially unexpectedly.

An upset is composed of three elements:

- Thwarted intention
- Unfulfilled expectation
- Undelivered communication

Vulnerable

1. Capable of being wounded or physically injured.
2. Open to criticism or attack.
3. Open to attack by armed forces.

Bibliography

Suggested Reading List

Ailes, Roger. *You Are the Message*. Homewood, IL: Dow Jones-Irwin, 1988.

Alpert, Richard (aka Das, Babba Ram). *Be Here Now*. New York: Crown Publishing, 1971.

Assagioli, Roberto. *Psychosynthesis*. New York: Penguin, 1976.

Bach, Richard. *Jonathan Livingston Seagull*. New York: MacMillan Co., 1970.

Bailey, Alice. *Ponder on This*. New York: Lucis Publishing Co., 1971.

Benner, Joseph. *The Impersonal Life*. San Gabriel, CA: Willing Publishing, 1971.

Benson, H. "The Relaxation Response" in *Mind-Body Medicine*. Yonkers, NY: Consumer Reports Books, 1993.

Brantley, Jeffrey. *Calming Your Anxious Mind*. Oakland, CA: New Harbinger Publications, 2007.

Brooks, Michael. *Instant Rapport*. New York: Warner Books, 1989.

Castaneda, Carlos. *A Separate Reality*. New York: Simon and Schuster, 1971.

————. *Journey to Ixtlan*. New York: Simon and Schuster, 1972.

————. *Teachings of Don Juan*. New York: Simon and Schuster, 1973.

Cohen, Alan. *The Dragon Doesn't Live Here Anymore*. Kula, HI: Alan Cohen Publications and Workshops, 1981.

Covey, Stephen R. *The 7 Habits of Highly Effective People*. New York: Simon and Schuster, 1989.

————. *First Things First*. New York: Simon and Schuster, 1994.

Crum, Thomas. *The Magic of Conflict*. New York: Simon and Schuster, 1987.

Emery, Stewart. *Actualizations*. New York: Doubleday and Co., 1978.

Gawain, Shakti. *Creative Visualization*. Berkeley, CA: Whatever Publishing, 1982.

Gibran, Kahlil. *The Prophet*. New York: Alfred A. Knopf, 1920.

Glass, Lillian. *Talk to Win*. New York: Putnam Publishing Group, 1987.

Golas, Thaddeus. *The Lazy Man's Guide to Enlightenment*. Palo Alto, CA: Seed Center, 1972.

Hesse, Herman. *Siddhartha*. New York: New Directions Publishing, 1957.

Hoff, Ron. *I Can See You Naked*. Kansas City, MO: Andrews McMeel, 1988.

Jampolsky, Gerald. *Love is Letting Go of Fear*. Berkeley, CA: Celestial Arts, 2004.

Jeffers, Susan. *Feel the Fear and Do it Anyway*. New York: Ballantine Books, 1987.

Keyes, Ken. *Handbook to Higher Consciousness*. Berkeley, CA: Living Love Center, 1975.

Linver, Sandy. *Speak Easy*. New York: Summit Books, 1978.

Loehr, James. *Mentally Tough*. New York: M. Evans and Company, 1986.

Nhat Hanh, Thich. *Breathe! You Are Alive*. Berkeley, CA: Parallax Press, 1996.

Peck, Scott. *The Road Less Traveled*. New York: Touchstone Books, 1978.

Peoples, David. *Presentations Plus*. New York: John Wiley & Sons, 1992.

Powers, Bob. *Instructor Excellence*. San Francisco, CA: Jossey-Bass, 1992.

Robbins, Anthony. *Unlimited Power*. New York: Fawcett-Columbine Publishers, 1986.

Ruiz, Don Miguel. *The Four Agreements*. San Rafael, CA: Amber-Allen Publishing, Inc., 1997.

Saraydarian, Torkom. *The Science of Becoming Oneself*. Reseda, CA: Aquarian Books, 1969.

Satprem. *Sri Aurobindo, or, The Adventure of Consciousness*. Pondicherry, India: Sri Aurobindo Society, 1968.

Shah, Idires. *Tales of the Dervishes*. New York: E.P. Dutton and Company, 1967.

Tolle, Eckhart. *Stillness Speaks*. Vancouver, BC, Canada: Namaste Publishing, 2003.

————. *The Power of Now*. Novato, CA: New World Library, 2004.

————. *A New Earth*. New York: Dutton, 2005.

Yogananda, Paramahansa. *The Autobiography of a Yogi*. Los Angeles, CA: Self-Realization Fellowship, 1998.

Index

audience (*continued*)
as a database, 9
deferring to the, 95, 104
definition of, 182
developing credibility with, 61
and developing the purpose,
48–53, 97
and enrollment in presentation,
53–55
keeping interested with trial
close, 57–58
key points for, 55–57, 62–65
knowledge of, 171–172
managing the conversation with,
69–81, 103, 159–165
nuking the, 9, 115
participation, 42, 152–157
paying attention. *see* attention,
audience paying
presenter understanding the, 50
questioning the, 135–157
as receivers of communication,
1–4
relationship, building with,
38–39, 41–42, 58–59, 65–66
remembering data, 3–5, 8, 33,
38, 45, 51
and removing psychological firewall, 30–43
resistance from, managing,
83–112
taking care of logistics for, 36,
59–61
as threat to presenter's survival,
24–27, 30
understanding data. *see* understanding data
auditory noise, 72
authority on subject matter, being
an, 41
awareness
conscious, 113–133
conversation expanding, 52

keeping during presentations,
72, 164
lack of behind firewall, 27
and managing resistance, 84, 94
of self, 29
state of, 23

B

Bailey, Alice, 11
bandwidth, 182, 185
barrier
and the art of questioning,
150
breaking through the firewall,
21–43
definition of, 182–183
and managing resistance, 95
and use of mass, 2, 95
and visual aids, 172
baud rate, 12, 183
being, 7, 87, 183
belief
and brain as a database, 22–24
breaking through the firewall,
36
and conscious awareness, 119–
120, 122–123, 125, 128
definition of, 183–184
and managing resistance, 89
and owning the room, 80
blame, 97, 184, 209
block, 26–27, 30, 109, 133, 172,
185
body
checks, 15–17, 72, 185
conscious awareness of, 114
and owning the room, 71–72,
76–79
relaxing during presentation,
13, 15–16, 164
and resistance, 84
and wireless packet delivery,
3–6, 8–9

body of a presentation, 62–64, 67, 176
bombs, dropping data, 9
bore/boring, 5, 46, 172, 185
brain, evolution of, 22
brainwashing, 129
breathing during presentation, 16, 80, 103
broadband connection
to audience, 5, 8, 12–13, 163
body as tool for, 72
confidence as, 25–26
conscious awareness as, 7, 113–133
definition of, 185
giving space to the moment, 106
grounded/anchored, 2, 5, 15, 72–73
IT presentation compared to, 2
pauses creating, 16–17
preference from audience, 31
business cards, collecting, 38, 109

C

call for action, 57–58, 63–64, 67, 176
Carnegie, Dale, 74
Carroll, Alan, 27, 29
cheerleader, being for audience, 163
clear, 7, 185
closed questions, 136–137, 139, 149
collision, 186
commitment, 4, 8–9, 27, 77, 107, 186–187
communication
and the art of questioning, 135–157
and building rapport, 161. see also relationship
conscious awareness of, 113–133
creating space for, 79–80
definition of, 187
delivering wholeheartedly, 9
and eye contact. see eye contact
firewalls as barriers to, 27, 31–32
IT presentation as, 1–2
and managing resistance, 89–91, 95–96, 98–104, 106–110, 112
and managing the conversation, 159–165
in present time, 12–13, 19
and presentation as a conversation, 45–67
strategies, 35–43
two-way, maintaining, 45, 159
undelivered, 106, 156, 214
use of body in, 3–6
communication packets
and body checks, 16, 72
creating space packets in between, 8, 13–17, 19, 72, 132, 164, 174
data in, 9
definition of, 187
effectiveness in firing, 33
IT presentation as, 1–4
lack of voice in, 6, 8
and Point of Focus, 73, 130–131
and resistance, 83–86
sending keep-alives with, 79
tennis ball representing a, 156
wireless process, 11–12
communion, 187. see also sharing
compassion, 85–86, 108, 157, 187–188
complete, 59, 122, 188
complex, 46
conclusion of a presentation, 64, 67, 176
confidence, 25–30, 41, 71–73, 81
congestion, 12, 188

consciousness
    awareness of, 113–133
    and body checks, 16
    and brain as a database, 23–24
    and connection with audience,
        8, 27, 42
    content, 12–13, 19, 115, 121,
        188
    developing, 29–31
    levels of, 7
    and managing resistance, 112
    universal, 86
conversation. *see also* presentation
    and the art of questioning,
        135–157
    creating space in the, 104
    definition of, 189
    leading the, 69–81, 103,
        159–165
    and managing resistance, 105,
        107, 109
    presentation as a, 35–43
    purpose to, establishing, 97–98
    structure of, 45–67
Copernicus, 93, 121, 128
corporate, deferring to, 102
courage, 25–30, 32–35, 189
Covey, Stephen, 90, 97
creation, 189. *see also* re-creating
    communication
credibility, 33, 40, 47, 50, 56, 61

D

data
    addiction, 13, 132
    additional in handouts, 65
    audience remembering, 3–5, 8,
        33, 45, 51
    and brain as a database, 26
    commitment to, 4, 8–9, 77
    communication of, 4
    conscious awareness of, 115–
        116, 119

delivering with confidence,
    41–42
and developing the purpose,
    47–49, 53
dropping into space, 19
dumpers, 2, 9, 11, 27, 33–34, 57,
    115, 119
firewalls as barriers to, 31,
    33–35
focusing too much on, 70, 132,
    144, 164
generation of, 16
ideal percentage in communica-
    tion packet, 3
IT presentation as, 2
in PowerPoint presentations,
    171–172, 176
quantity vs. quality of, 56–57,
    115
resistance based on, 84, 86
understanding. *see* understand-
    ing data
use of in presentations, 2–4, 9,
    11–13
Data Land
    and the art of questioning, 153
    avoiding by using pauses, 132
    being in when hiding behind
        firewalls, 27
    and conscious awareness, 119,
        164
    definition of, 189
    focus on content as being in,
        115–116, 163
    as lowest level of consciousness,
        7, 13
    and no awareness in body, 72
    no concern for audience while
        in, 57
    and Point of Focus, 131
databases
    of audience members, 9, 138,
        140–141, 143, 146

power (*continued*)
  and developing the purpose, 47
  increasing with Point of Focus, 73
  on offense, 26
  and removing psychological firewall, 30–31, 41
The Power of Now, 97, 105
PowerPoint presentations
  additional tools for, 62–63, 66, 95
  avoiding facing slides, 75
  breaking through the firewall, 34
  challenge of, 171–177
  and controlling physical space, 70
  and developing the purpose, 51–52
  as exterior data, 115
  introduction of, 53–54
  making interesting, 59
  not exciting, 163
  structure of, 66–67
  use of sound in, 78
  and wireless packet delivery, 2, 9, 16
praise, 97, 206, 209
preframing slides, 173–174
presence, state of, 23, 114
present time. *see also* time
  avoiding purposeless movement in the, 71–72
  confidence as being in the, 25–26, 29, 31–32
  conscious awareness during, 114–128
  definition of, 206–207
  and enrollment in presentation, 53
  and level of consciousness, 7
  and managing resistance, 97, 106

practicing skill of staying in the, 80
staying in with audience, 12–13, 19, 57, 163–164
presentation. *see also* conversation
  after the, 42–43, 65
  before the day of the, 35–36
  body of the, 62–64, 67, 176
  conclusion of the, 64, 67, 176
  conscious awareness during the, 113–133
  during the, 39–42
  as a conversation, 45–67, 159
  day of the, 36–39
  during the, 39–42
  introduction of, 47–62, 66–67, 97–98, 139, 164, 174–175
  as a team sport, 136, 146
prison, 7
Private Branch Exchange (PBX), 141–142
protocol, 22, 182, 207
provoke, 195, 207
psychological firewall, 21–22, 25–28, 30–43, 96
psychology, 90, 114, 117–130, 140
purpose
  and the art of questioning, 147
  definition of, 47, 207–208
  developing the, 47–53, 55, 59, 63–64, 66–67, 175–176
  of knowledge, 121, 127
  and managing resistance, 97–98
  and managing the conversation, 162–164
  modulating voice with, 73–75
  moving body with, 72

Q

questions
  and answer sessions, 63–64, 67, 81, 176
  art of asking, 135–137

the**broadband**connection

• • • **228** • • •

index

suppress, 212

surrender, 105, 112, 123, 126–127, 212–213

survival
and conditioning of the mind, 128
and creating a safe space, 160
definition of, 213
and expression of emotion, 74
firewalls as means of, 22, 24–25, 31
and managing resistance, 84, 91
and mind creating time, 119, 121, 127

synchronization, 213

voice
   tone of, 73–75, 79, 84, 143
   use of in presentations, 2–3,
      5–6, 8–9, 11
Voice over IP, 52, 55, 61, 137, 141–
   142, 153, 175. *see also* Internet
   Protocol (IP)
vulnerability, 25–26, 29, 31–33, 41,
   74, 98, 214

W

The Way of Transformation, 25
weaknesses in solution, preparing
   for, 101–102
whiteboards
   and logistics, 60
   and managing resistance, 95,
      102
   and owning the room, 70, 75
   and structure of presentation,
      66–67
   varying media tools using, 63
   as visual aids, 170–171

in wireless packet delivery, 2
WIIIFM (What Is In It For Me)
   and audience paying attention,
      78, 162
   in conclusion, 64
   and enrollment in presentation,
      53–54
   key points, use of, 56
   and managing resistance, 111
   and PowerPoint presentations,
      66–67, 171
   purpose, developing the, 66–67
wireless packet delivery, 1–19
witness, self as, 23–24
word symbols, 18
writing down questions, 102

Y

You Are the Message, 69, 103

Z

Zen, 30, 117

About Alan Carroll

Engaging and incisive, Alan Carroll is one of the pre-eminent authorities worldwide on teaching IT professionals the art of public speaking. A transpersonal psychologist who has combined his clinical study of the human mind with his natural talent as a speaker, he travels around the globe at the behest of such influential corporations as Cisco Systems, Lucent, Nortel, Avaya, and Symantec Corporation, among many others, to work with their IT personnel.

Cleverly utilizing vernacular and principles specific to the IT industry in his training and coaching sessions, he has helped thousands of IT professionals worldwide evolve from nervous, insecure speakers into savvy, successful presenters. From struggling third-world countries to prosperous European cities, Carroll's innovative approach to training IT professionals how to connect with live audiences and turn abstract concepts into compelling conversation continues to impact the careers of thousands.

Carroll, whose travel schedule often has him flying from the farthest reaches of the globe, frequently having to hit two or three different continents within a matter of days or weeks, will tell anyone who asks that, despite being away from home and family for long periods, it's worth it to be able to watch his students unleash the graceful speaker hidden within each of them.

Alan Carroll earned both his BA and MS in psychology at San Jose State University. A licensed psychologist with thirty years' experience motivating human behavior, he is the principal in Alan Carroll and Associates. He lives in Stonington, Connecticut, with his wife Donna and two children Alan and Jennifer.

To contact Alan Carroll:

E-mail: aecarroll@earthlink.net
Phone: +1-408-356-1892
Web Site: www.carrolltrain.com

Alan Carroll and Associates

Alan Carroll and Associates is an international training and consulting group that has delivered transformational workshops and training programs in over fifty different countries throughout the world and specializes in the areas of communication and presentation skills. We may be reached via e-mail at aecarroll@earthlink.net, via voice mail at +1-408-356-1892, and through our Web site at www.carrolltrain.com.